LIFE BENEATH THE SURFACE

Mike Pilavachi
with Craig Borlase

Regal

From Gospel Light
Ventura, California, U.S.A.

PUBLISHED BY REGAL BOOKS
FROM GOSPEL LIGHT
VENTURA, CALIFORNIA, U.S.A.
Regal PRINTED IN THE U.S.A.

Regal Books is a ministry of Gospel Light, a Christian publisher dedicated to serving the local church. We believe God's vision for Gospel Light is to provide church leaders with biblical, user-friendly materials that will help them evangelize, disciple and minister to children, youth and families.

It is our prayer that this Regal book will help you discover biblical truth for your own life and help you meet the needs of others. May God richly bless you.

For a free catalog of resources from Regal Books/Gospel Light, please call your Christian supplier or contact us at 1-800-4-GOSPEL or www.regalbooks.com.

All Scripture quotations, unless otherwise indicated, are taken from the *Holy Bible, New International Version*®. Copyright © 1973, 1978, 1984 by International Bible Society. Used by permission of Zondervan Publishing House. All rights reserved.

Other versions used are
KJV—King James Version. Authorized King James Version.
NKJV—Scripture taken from the *New King James Version*. Copyright © 1979, 1980, 1982 by Thomas Nelson, Inc. Used by permission. All rights reserved.

This edition issued by special arrangement with Hodder and Stoughton Limited of 338 Euston Road, London NW1 3BH, England. Original title: *Live the Life*.
Revised and updated edition published by Regal Books in 2006.

Library of Congress Cataloging-in-Publication Data
Pilavachi, Mike.
   Life beneath the surface / Mike Pilavachi, with Craig Borlase.— Rev. and updated ed.
      p. cm.
   Rev. ed. of: Live the life. 1998.
   ISBN 0-8307-3897-5 (trade paper)
   1. Christian life. I. Borlase, Craig. II. Pilavachi, Mike. Live the life. III. Title.

BV4501.3.P545 2006
248.4—dc22   2005030666

1   2   3   4   5   6   7   8   9   10   /   10   09   08   07   06

For additional information, visit www.gospellightworldwide.org; write to Gospel Light Worldwide, P.O. Box 3875, Ventura, CA 93006; or send an e-mail to info@gospellightworldwide.org.

To Andrew Croft
Thank you for all you have taught me about
leadership and what it means to pursue Jesus.
I hope I can repay the debt.

CONTENTS

PART 3: GO

ACKNOWLEDGMENTS

We would like to thank a number of our friends who have helped us in the writing of this book: Elspeth Taylor, who had the original idea and has been a constant encouragement since; Andi Smith and Dave Baxter, who so accurately typed the transcripts; Andrew Latimer for help and advice well beyond the call of duty; Matt Redman, David Pytches, Emma Mitchell, Mark Stibbe, Martyn and Emily Layzell, who read the manuscript and made many wise and helpful comments. We would like to thank Emma Borlase, who is wife to one of us and friend to both, and whose thoughts can be found by the discerning in various parts of this book. Last but not least, we would like to thank our church, Soul Survivor Watford. Many of the thoughts and ideas in this book have been learned in this community and many of the stories are about you. Sorry.

INTRODUCTION

Something is happening in the Church. It used to be that people, especially young people, were fighting to get out, but today they're coming back. Everywhere we go we see a generation with a new passion for Jesus. We see generations rising up with a radical commitment to living the life. This book is written to encourage all those who want to go deeper with God and even further out into the world.

Because preparation is everything, *Life Beneath the Surface* tries to help with the business of getting to grips with the hows and the whys of Christian living. Taking it in three practical chunks, we first of all sink our pre-molars into getting ready: looking at the roots of our relationship with God. Then we move on to examine how we make sure we're steady: both in ourselves and in our relationships with others. Finally we rinse out with a look at the ways we can respond to a simple instruction: Go.

This book is best read with a Bible nearby. As you find Scriptures weaving in and out, you will want to check them for yourself. It is important to integrate God's teaching into every aspect of our lives.

God is calling His people to go beyond the caramel coating of life. There is a need today for people who will meet with Him and who will want Him to reach every aspect of their lives. "Worship" and "obedience" are good words and fine qualities for us to take on. If our worship really takes us deeper with God, it will also take us further out into the world. In obedience we will deny ourselves, take up our cross and follow Him, obeying Him with all our lives.

Mike Pilavachi
Craig Borlase

Part 1:
GETTING READY

MAKING FRIENDS WITH GOD
(It all begins with friendship)

I got out my ruler and drew a thick red line underneath the title "Why I Am Not a Christian." I had just spent 600 words annihilating one of the five major world religions, and I felt good. The way I saw it, Christianity was for the old, the weak and the stupid. My essay explained it all perfectly, and anyone who read it would be forced to:

1. agree,
2. say that I was a 14-year-old genius, and
3. give me an A+ and let me off cross-country for the rest of the term.

Things didn't go quite as I planned, and I later found out that 40 years before me someone else had also written an essay with the same title, but his was much better as he had a beard and was a philosopher called Bert. The other bizarre thing is that exactly one year after I had put pen to paper, I decided to spend the rest of my life doing whatever Jesus wanted me to do. Being a Christian—I had discovered—was not about following a set of rules, but about something far more powerful and exciting: friendship.

Life begins with friendship. God decided that it would be good to share things, so He spent a busy six days in the workshop. Later, once we had managed to completely miss the point about God, Jesus came down to reunite us to Him. Finally, the Holy Spirit was promised so that we might continue to be close to God, even after Jesus was crucified, rose again and went to heaven. God wants us to be His friends. In John 15:12-15, Jesus says something amazing after He told the disciples that the Holy Spirit was on His way:

> My command is this: Love each other as I have loved you. Greater love has no one than this, that he lay down his life for his friends. You are my friends if you do what I command. I no longer call you servants, because a servant does not know his master's business. Instead, I have called you friends, for everything that I learned from my Father I have made known to you.

The disciples were Jesus' friends. They weren't servants, slaves or paid companions there to make Him feel popular; they were all mates. Friendship is nothing if we don't let people see what we're really like, and Jesus made sure that they knew everything that He had learned from His Father. He wept in front of them and told them about the things that made Him happy and the things that made Him sad.

The History of Friendship

Friendship is a relationship. Way back when He was surrounded by lots of nothing, God decided to create the human race—people who would be like Him—so that He could have relationship. He said "Let us make man in our own image, in our likeness" (Gen. 1:26) and got on with the business of making people He could love. Throughout the Old Testament we follow a story that has one main theme: God, the maker of heaven and Earth, yearning for a relationship with Israel, the people with whom He had made a special pact.

The arrangement we have that is most similar to the pact God made with Israel is marriage. Back then, Israel agreed to love and obey their maker, and in return God would love, protect and care for them. This covenant was a unique agreement, but it broke God's heart as Israel constantly fell short, turning away from a friendship with Almighty God. You see something of God's sorrow in the book of Hosea, where God told the prophet Hosea to marry a prostitute called Gomer. Hosea stuck by her and stayed faithful, but she carried on sleeping around (it says she lifted her skirt to every passing man). Thus, Hosea and God had something in common: The people they loved did not keep their promises. God told Hosea to say to the nation that they were little more than a whore, because they were unfaithful.

God's pain at this broken relationship was real, but He didn't leave it there. He sent Jesus to become like His creation so that His creation might once again become like Him. Jesus became a man to take away the disease called sin, which had separated us from friendship with God. By dying on the cross, Jesus told us that we can be forgiven, that we can be friends with God again. None of this would be possible if God didn't first love us, and our relationship is based on our response to God's love for us, as John was keen to point out:

> Dear friends, let us love one another, for love comes from God. Everyone who loves has been born of God and knows God. Whoever does not love does not know God, because God is love. This is how God showed his love among us: He sent his one and only Son into the world that we might live through him. This is love: not that we loved God, but that he loved us and sent his Son as an atoning sacrifice for our sins (1 John 4:7-10).

Like the ceiling of the Sistine Chapel, where Michelangelo painted God's hand stretched out to touch the hand of man, it is God who sets the ball rolling. Our role is to respond to His love, to the mercy He showed us when He sacrificed His Son. Our worship, our prayer, our reading of the Bible, our caring for the poor and our telling others about Him all come as a response to His call to us. Christianity is all about knowing Jesus and being children of the Father, knowing Him through the forgiveness of His Son.

We see pictures of this all the way through the Scriptures. In John 17:3, in His great high priestly prayer, Jesus says:

Now this is eternal life: that they might know you, the only true God, and Jesus Christ, whom you have sent.

Eternal life is not going to Mars and turning left, passing through a hole in the space/time continuum. Eternal life is about a relationship with God, and this physical life is all about getting to know each other beforehand. Bearing in mind that this is why God made us, it is the most natural, normal thing that we as human beings can do. Because we were made by Him and for Him, our worship is vital and important because it is an expression of our love for Him.

A wonderful book in the Old Testament that works out the idea of this love relationship is Song of Songs. Christians have found it hard to know what to make of this book over the years, feeling that because it follows the progress of a love affair between two people, it might not be suitable for the Church. It has been a bit of a favorite of mine, although at first I liked it just because it used the word "breasts" more than once. Thankfully there is a bit more to it than snigger material for young boys, and it comes out as a great picture of the love affair between God and His people.

It is important to note that this is not a love affair of equals, but it's actually about a king and his maiden. In the same way, we are not the equals of God. When we're called the friends of God, when the Bible calls the Church the Bride of Christ, we are most definitely not the leader. After all,

"The LORD confides in those who fear him" (Ps. 25:14). We have a friendship with Almighty God, not a pet poodle. In this way, knowing that God is the boss takes the pressure off. If the friendship depended on our being good enough, we'd all be very, very alone.

Yes, but God Doesn't Love Me

This may all sound fine in theory, but for many of us, getting around to believing that God's love is for us is about as easy as believing that God has a bus pass. Look around us and there are plenty of examples of how God loves, cares and yearns for His people. But look inside us and there's little more than a bad smell and a load of broken promises. If you've been a Christian for a while, you might have just about convinced yourself that God loves you, but that He only loves you because He has to—and that really, whenever He thinks of you, He is totally unimpressed.

I love the passage where Jesus was baptized by John the Baptist and as He came out of the water a voice came from heaven saying, "This is my son, whom I love; with him I am well pleased" (Matt 3:17). Can you imagine how great it must have been to have God publicly shouting from the skies, "This is my son—I love Him; I'm pleased with Him." Sometimes I go into a little fantasy and imagine myself with a group of people when all of a sudden God clears His throat and points His biggest and most God-like finger down at me.

"That Mike Pilavachi is all right," He says, His booming voice shattering windows. "I quite like Him."

Then I imagine how everyone's attitude about me would change. People would drop their shopping bags and point at me. "Wow," they would say, "Mike Pilavachi; he's God's boy." If that happened, I'd have T-shirts printed up that recounted the whole heavenly message every time I entered a room. Of course, the truly amazing thing is that it has happened (not the part about the T-shirt); God has said that He likes me and loves me. Maybe it hasn't been quite the publicity stunt I would have planned, but through Jesus He said it loud and clear. Jesus didn't have to earn God's love, and what God says about Jesus, His Son, He says about me and about you. God has said that He loves, likes and cares for each one of us.

Another reason lots of us have for finding it hard to believe in God's love is that our own experience with our fathers has been rough. Lots of us find it hard to believe that God could be such a good friend because our friends have let us down. What's the solution to all this? We need to get deeply into the Bible, because it's there we find the truth about God. As we read the Bible, we hear God speaking to us through the stories of His relationship with others. What's more, the Holy Spirit takes the words of the Bible and feeds them into our hearts, acting like a kind of high-grade spiritual fertilizer. That's why it is good to meditate on God's Word, taking time to think over the words.

Believing That He Does Love Me

One of my favorite passages to meditate on comes from a little book at the end of the Old Testament. It's one of the minor prophets, Zephaniah, but don't let that put you off.

The Lord your God is with you, he is mighty to save. He will take great delight in you, he will quiet you with his love, he will rejoice over you with singing (Zeph. 3:17).

In the past, I've written this verse down and looked at it every day, feeding on the goodness it contains. I usually take it slowly, one line at a time:

The Lord your God is with you.

If you are a Christian, have given your life to Jesus and have made a commitment to Him, then the Lord your God is with you. That means He isn't just there for you on Sundays, but the rest of the time too. When it gets to Monday morning and it's time to get back to school, college or work, it might be harder to feel, but it's true—He's with you. And not just tagging along, asking to be looked after either . . .

He is mighty to save.

We need to remember that we have a powerful God with us, one who can make a difference to our lives. Imagine that you are walking with me down a dark alley late at night when a bunch of particularly violent-looking thugs appears from the other end of the alley. They stop us and begin to harass us. You're frightened and weigh my chances: four violent men against me—the pastor who cries whenever one of his potted plants dies. You do the only sensible thing and run away.

Now imagine that you're walking down that dark alley with Mike Tyson at your side (in the days when he could win fights). Instead of staring at the floor and crossing your legs, you may have a bit of a swagger as the gang of four approaches. If they ask if you want to make something of it, you might reply, "Yes, I would like to make something of it." Then you could turn to Mike and tell him to eat as many of their ears as he wanted. God, in that situation, is more like Mike Tyson than Mike Pilavachi. God is mighty to save and big enough to make a difference in anybody's life. Whether it's saving us from our own sins or stepping in with miracles or guidance, God has the power.

He will take great delight in you.

By the time my meditation gets around to this bit, I'm usually getting hungry. Strangely, this helps as I take great delight in food, so it gives me an idea of how God feels about me. Just like me when I'm served up a full Greek meal, God becomes ecstatic when He thinks about us. He loves it when we meet together to worship Him, and He loves it when we talk to Him on our own. To know that God loves to hear my prayers is a great inspiration for me to pray. It helps me to know that He reacts to my prayers and makes me think of it as being a conversation.

He will quiet you with his love.

I finally understood some of the meaning of this promise when I was browsing my way through the cheese section of my local supermarket. Somewhere around the garlic roule I saw a five-year-old boy looking miserable. Knowing that I didn't have much of a taste for garlic at that age either, I thought nothing of it and went back to my research. Soon he began to sniff and I realized what was going on. A lady came up to him and asked if he was lost. At that, he started to bawl his eyes out, accompanying it with the sort of piercing sound that only five-year-old boys can make. Eventually an announcement came over the loudspeaker system: "Would the mother of a little boy who answers to the name of 'aaaaarh' please collect him from the soft cheese section?"

Soon, the boy's mum was there, cuddling him and telling him that everything was all right. The boy kept on crying, but his mum kept holding him, telling him that she loved him and wasn't going away. This carried on for some time until the boy stopped crying. His mum had made him still, peaceful and secure again with her love. She quieted him with her love. Most of us may not cry on the outside like that five-year-old boy, but we've been so hurt and broken by things that have happened to us that we're crying on the inside. God says that He can be there for us. He will hold us close and quiet us with His love.

He will rejoice over you with singing.

I always thought it was our job to rejoice over Him with singing, not His job to rejoice over us. Partly it is up to us to thank Him for who He is and what He has done, but while we do that, He goes wild over us. The Hebrew phrase that translates as "rejoice over you with singing" can be translated to mean "to spin like a top and let out whoops of joy." It amazes me that God does that for each one of us.

This verse from Zephaniah perfectly contains the message of Christianity. God is alive, forgiving, interested, compassionate, loving and worthy of praise. This is the beginning of life. If we understand the truth of this, if we let it seep into our souls' roots, we will find ourselves living the most outrageously full life imaginable. If not, it's all just meaningless rules.

A few years ago I went on a trip to the Isle of Man to have a few meetings. Matt Redman and I stayed with a family who had three boys, the youngest of which was a six-month-old baby named Ben. As Matt, Ben and I sat at the dinner table waiting for the indigestion to fade, I was playing with Ben. Being a cuddly kind of guy, I know all the moves, and I showed him my full repertoire. I bounced a little, made noises, hung him upside down and balanced him on my chin, when suddenly I sensed something brewing in his diaper region. Immediately, I held him at arm's length, twisting my head this way and that to avoid the smell. My arms soon started to hurt, so I passed him over to Matt. He soon figured out what was going on with the kid's diaper, and before long he too was holding him as far away from his body as possible. Ben started to cry, unhappy at the combination of soggy diaper and stretched out upper body. His mum came in and took hold of him, cuddling him as close to her as she could, unfazed by the smell or the mess he had created.

God, I realized, does exactly the same thing with us. When we're tired and miserable, unable to look after ourselves, and having all sorts of problems, God pulls us in close. Ultimately, that's where He wants us—next to His heart.

THERE WAS A NUN, A DONKEY AND A GREEK BLOKE . . .
(A chapter about worship)

It's strange the way things change with the seasons. The summer of 1997 saw 10,000 people jumping up and down to a country western inspired tune with lyrics that went "Na na na na na na, hey!" It was the soundtrack to that year's Soul Survivor festival, and as I watched the heaving hoards I asked myself a fundamental question: *What on Earth does this have in common with that old classic "All Things Bright and Beautiful"? Are they related? Can they really both be worship? What is worship anyway?*

According to the Bible, to worship our Father is our highest calling; nothing that we can do pleases God more. The Old Testament is full of examples of how, for the Israelites, the biggest battle was always who or what were they going to worship. There was never a question of whether they were going to worship; it was part of their nature—and the choice was always between worshiping God and worshiping idols. The bottom line for us today is exactly the same; the basic nature of humanity is to worship, so what are we going to focus on? For those of us who have chosen to worship the likes of the New York Yankees, the Republican Party, Manchester United or ourselves, there is but one antidote—to worship God.

The book of Jeremiah contains a potent verse in which God proclaims, "My people have committed two sins: They have forsaken me, the spring of living water, and have dug their own cisterns, broken cisterns that cannot hold water" (2:13). This is the heart of the matter, the core of broken humanity: When we abandon God, turning away from relationship with Him, we choose second best.

What Is Worship?

Worship is the ultimate expression of relationship with God. Worship is coming home. As the saying goes, within each of us lies a God-shaped hole—one that cannot be filled by religious ritual, but only by a living relationship with Him.

The word most often used in the New Testament for worship (66 times in all) is the Greek word *proskuneo*, which can be translated to mean "to come towards to kiss." It means to come to a place of tenderness, to touch the heart of God and to allow Him to touch our hearts. Worship is praise; worship is celebration; worship is intercession; but worship, ultimately, is adoration. As in the deepest of relationships, the most intimate place is the one where we can cherish and express our love for each other. The socializing and the chatting all lead to the place of adoration. To worship God is our duty, and it is the greatest commandment that Jesus gave: Love the Lord your God with all your heart, soul, mind and strength (see Mark 12:30). That we love God with all that we have and all that we are is the ultimate act of humanity.

The centuries-old Westminster Shorter Catechism was written in a question and answer format to give expression to the major doctrines of the Christian faith. Question number one gets stuck right in with "What is the chief end of man?" Instead of replying that it is the head or the feet, the people let it rip with "The chief end of man is to glorify God and enjoy Him forever." This is our main function in life and presents Jesus' greatest commandment in another way: Our object in life is to glorify God and enjoy Him forever. In other words, we are to worship Him!

How Do We Worship?

Thankfully (especially considering my innovative approach to vocal tuning), worship is more than just singing. Worship is about the whole of our life. If our songs and our instruments are doing one thing and our lives are doing another, it is a stench in God's nostrils. "Away with the noise of your songs," He says in Amos 5:23, if we are not living lives that match up to the words. Matching up our words and our lives is one heck of a big job; for if we are planning on adoring God, we are going to end up with a pretty long list of things to adore.

At the end of the day, worship cannot be separated from the marks of His character: justice, purity, mercy, compassion and truth. If we are going to have relationship with Him, we have to be prepared to explore the extreme breadth of His character, to find the ways of expressing His nature in every aspect of our lives.

One of the words used in the Old Testament for "worship" was the Hebrew verb *abad,* which can be translated "to work." Even today, the Jews regard their work as part of worship—the whole of their lives are to be given over to God, not only what is done on the Sabbath or during prayer times, but also what is done in the classroom, office or on the factory floor. Jesus illustrated this at the end of Matthew's gospel:

> "For I was hungry and you gave me something to eat, I was thirsty and you gave me something to drink, I was a stranger and you invited me in, I needed clothes and you clothed me, I was sick and you looked after me, I was in prison and you came to visit me." Then the righteous will answer him, "Lord, when did we see you hungry and feed you, or thirsty and give you something to drink? When did we see you a stranger and invite you in, or needing clothes and clothe you? When did we see you sick or in prison and go to visit you?" The King will reply, "I tell you the truth, whatever you did for one of the least of these brothers of mine, you did for me" (Matt. 25:35-40).

If we can learn to see worship as the way we relate to one another and not just to God while at church, we stand the chance of making real differences to the lives with which we come into contact. When Mother Teresa was asked why she served the poor, she wrapped up the whole gospel by answering that it was because she loved God.

We will return to worship as a way of life later in the chapter, but for now we turn to worship in song. There seems to be a special place given in the Bible to God's people meeting together and worshiping with music. The psalms are the Christian's handbook of this corporate worship. Many of the songs we sing today come straight from the psalms.

David wrote many of these psalms as an act of worship that was to be set to music, expressing love, reverence, praise and thanksgiving to God, but without ignoring life's pain, confusion and questions. Worship is not only an expression of our desire to follow God and imitate His character through our deeds, but it is also about bringing all of these other things to God. Often, music is the ideal medium through which to express these complex emotions, for there is something about music that touches the human heart. If bands like Coldplay can express the moods of our time through lyrics and attitude, then surely we also can use music to express a passionate love for God.

As an afro-sporting teenager in North London, my trips to the lower end of my mood swings were often accompanied by the music of Simon and Garfunkel. When they sang, "I am a rock, I am an island," I was there, belting it out with all the passion that my soul could muster. I had the words written out on a card and read them whenever I was feeling low. "Yes," I'd say, "that is how I feel. I touch no one and no one touches me." The words became my chant, and even though this particular island did cry and this rock did feel pain, I sang them with passion. Whenever I hear this song today, I immediately find myself back in my room, with its orange and brown wallpaper and me, ready to take on the world.

Another powerful aspect of music and worship is that it brings people together. Way back when Solomon was king, overseeing the building of the Temple, there were times when the musicians and the singers would get together and do their thing. The result was not some mildly relaxing mood-inducement—on the contrary, the glory of the Lord, His very essence, descended. The Bible notes that many people would take part in these times, which is important because it reinforces the point made in Hebrews that we should not neglect meeting together (see Heb. 10:25) as each of us has "psalms, hymns and spiritual songs" (Eph. 5:19) that we can contribute to the overall adoration of our Maker. The glory of the Lord descends when we offer ourselves to Him in worship (see 2 Chron. 7).

Even though it is confusing at times, it appears that the advice to "not forsake meeting together" is pretty sound and is worth sticking by. At Soul Survivor, there have been times in our meetings when we were worshiping God and suddenly felt that His glory had descended. It is not surprising then that many of us have been healed during times of worship. Because worship is all about relationship with God, it makes sense that the time we spend with Him results in Him rubbing off on us, inspiring us to become more like Him. In fact, it is often during the most intimate of moments that we can become inspired and feel the passion to do something practical, to worship through our lives.

But what if the services or meetings available to you aren't five-star worship bonanzas? Isn't it a little hard when the rest of the church doesn't understand and prefers things "the old way"? Unfortunately, there is a discipline in worship, which many of us need to learn again. Often, when we have been involved in new and exciting things, we forget that the songs themselves are unimportant; what matters is the heart. The decision to worship God whether we like the style or not is an act of spiritual discipline. The more alien we find the style, the greater the discipline.

Furthermore, we evangelicals seem to do a fairly good job of keeping up with the Joneses when it comes to the secular world. These days, this is marked by a mind-numbingly fast turnaround of style and information. What was *in* last summer was probably *out* by September, and what was news first thing Monday was worldwide and fully downloadable by the time Monday's midmorning coffee was just beginning to get cold. Cultural relevance is another chapter, but as a pre-meal snack ask yourself this question: Do we have to be slaves to the evolution of cool worship?

Worship is linked to a strange thing called anointing. Jesus was actually called the Anointed One. To have an anointing for worship, as to have an anointing for healing, is in a sense to have something of Jesus there. At times, worship can seem like a ritual; at the end, you might think that it was technically good (the band was in tune, in time or, depending on how fussy you are, was not wearing lycra), but maybe people didn't touch the heart of God. The good piece of news, though, is that even if the rest of the congregation isn't engaging with God, there is nothing to stop us from going for it. We are called to find Jesus in nature, in our meditations and amongst the poor—we surely ought to be able to find Him in a church that worships in a different way.

What Are the Benefits of Worship?

When we worship, we are healed. The *King James Version* of Psalm 22:3 says that the Lord inhabits the praises of His people; when we truly worship, it is as if we are touching the heart of God. It reminds me of the woman who reached out to touch Jesus in the crowd, believing that if she could just touch the hem of His garment, she would be healed (see Luke 8:44). For me, the most intimate of worship times gets me close to God, close enough that sometimes my own pain can be healed. The greatest emotional and spiritual healing has come when I have been worshiping God. I have wept before Him in worship in a way I would never have done at any other time and have ended up finding peace in my soul and feeling reoriented.

I once stood next to a nun at a meeting. It was still in the early days as far as "the worship movement" goes, and like the nun, I had traveled quite a way to reach that evening's meeting. The meeting began with an introduction and was swiftly followed by the main event: 13.5 minutes of uninterrupted worship. Pure bliss. Song after song came at us—"Joy Is the Flag," "Michael Row Your Boat Ashore"—all done with the proper instruments and everything. The band hit the home straight running, turning out a particularly fervent rendition of "Come Bless the Lord" that ended in a spontaneous round of applause. Man, we were on fire. Unfortunately, the old nun must have been a little deaf, for she carried on clapping. She had this serene expression on her face, and I was just about to give her a shove when she stopped and looked around.

"I suppose you're all wondering why I carried on clapping?" she asked, blushing a little. "You see, my hands have been paralyzed with arthritis for years, but as we were worshiping I forgot all about it, and look, I'm healed!"

What the nun found out was that worship is about taking our eyes off of ourselves and fixing them on the Lord. While Jesus distracts us so that we're no longer looking at ourselves, the Holy Spirit often sneaks up and heals us.

As well as healing us physically and emotionally, the Lord often speaks to us during times of worship, sometimes calling us to repentance. At one of the Soul Survivor meetings, a long line of people formed at the front during the worship. Thinking that they were about to complain, I got ready to apologize for the poor quality of the singer, when the first one pulled out a knife. I contemplated making a run for it, but I quickly realized that they were younger and faster. So I went closer and prepared to become Saint Mike Pilavachi, the Soul Survivor martyr.

"Can you get rid of this for me?" asked knife-boy.

"Why?" I asked him (we Greeks are born with an acute sense of mistrust).

"God told me to," he replied.

Each of his friends then came up and gave me their weapons. While I was obviously excited that God had done a wonderful thing in their lives, I must admit to feeling a little suspicious as to why they attended a Christian conference with enough weaponry to start a small military coup. For the rest of the week, whenever I passed them I made sure they kept their hands above their heads where I could see them.

How Does Worship Relate to a Church Service?

The worship time should be a possible focus for repentance, healing and unity, but it should also reflect and inspire the very direction in which the church is moving. When the Vineyard movement started, people would meet in a house, sing songs to Jesus and cry. They were hurting people who found that worship was the best way of carrying on a relationship with God. At Soul Survivor, we feel similar and consider worship to be our highest value and our first priority. It is neither the warm-up nor the wind-down; it is, in fact, the main event of our gatherings.

Worship has always been at the heart of the church service, and at our church we try to keep the preaching and the singing aspects of worship flowing together. Matt Redman, Tim Hughes, Martyn Layzell, Vicky Beeching and many others have been our minstrels. We may talk about a theme and the next thing you know Matt has written a song about it. As painful as it is for me to admit, I am sure that God has taught more people through the songs than through my sermons—people don't sing my sermons in the shower, but they do sing the songs.

One example of this is Matt's song "I'm Coming Back to the Heart of Worship."[1] We realized at Soul Survivor Watford in the autumn of 1996 that we had gotten so into the music for a while that we were missing the point of the whole thing. We had become lethargic and were relying on the music to take us into a place of supernatural fireworks. We had missed that heart of worship: relationship with Jesus. To try to sort this out, we banned the music and the musicians, sat on the floor, and just let anyone who wanted to start up a song do so. We had to ask each other what sacrifice of praise we brought and how hungry we were to pursue our relationship with God. We had to learn through times of pain that no matter what the setting, worship is about us and Jesus.

As a church, this became the most profound song that we knew. It reminded, encouraged and warned us about the core of our relationship with God. Again we knew that worship was not self-indulgence, but giving our hearts to Him.

The job of the worship leader is to lead the people into God's presence so that they can give Him His worth-ship (which is kind of like a ship, but full of all the good things that God deserves). The job of the worship leader is always to draw attention to Jesus and never to draw attention to himself or herself by performing.

There was a donkey that returned home one day, particularly flushed with excitement (I say "particularly" because he had always been a fairly excitable donkey).

"Mum," the donkey said, "you'll never guess what happened to me today. It was fantastic. I was just minding my own business, tied to a gatepost, and these two men came and got me. They led me down the street and everyone came out of their houses and they were all cheering me and clapping, and they were putting their cloaks in front of me, and they were tearing the branches off the trees and waving them at me, putting them on the ground in front of me. Mum . . . [big pause] I was famous! They did all this for your little donkey son—it was wonderful."

"Oh, my little donkey boy," replied his mum when he had calmed down a little. "When they were clapping and cheering and throwing the branches on the ground, they weren't doing it for you, they were doing it for the one you were carrying."

At the risk of sounding like a nagging parent myself, that is exactly what I keep on saying to our worship leaders: "Remember, you are only the donkey. It's the One you're carrying who is important."

The Whole Picture

To return to the wider concept of worship, it seems to me that worship through music is the activity of the Church gathered, while worship as a way of life is the activity of the Church scattered. The Church needs to be active when it is meeting together, just as it needs to be active during the other six days of the week. If we favor one over another, we lose the balance that is so crucial to our faith. The words without the actions are worse than irrelevant—they are actively despised by God. Equally, the works without the communication do not make for a relationship with God.

This is not to say that we Christians have the monopoly on good works—I believe that someone holding another belief can bring justice into the world. To the homeless person, a roof over his or her head is the same whether it comes from an atheist or a Christian. The difference is that we have to go and work amongst the "poor"; it is part of the deal. When we serve the poor and do good, we do it for God, drawing closer to Him and further away from our comforts.

As we try to fulfill our part of the bargain in this way, doing it for His sake, we tune in to His compassion. Our own compassion can become tired and even distorted, but at least with God we have a chance to continually return to the source of all compassion, the source of all goodness.

John 12 contains the most profound description of worship that I know. As Martha busied herself with the arrangements, Mary Magdalene poured a jar full of perfume over Jesus' feet, wiping them with her hair. The perfume itself was worth over a year's wages, and the act offended Judas, who was the light-fingered keeper of the money. He complained about the waste, about the fact that at his feet was a puddle of smelly liquid worth over 18 grand, and he was right. It was the most extravagant act of adoration, and it remains the best model of worship that we can find. Worship is wasting ourselves on God. It may start with singing a song, but before long it invades our money, our time, our talents and the rest of our lives. The key to the story comes at the end of verse 3, which says that "the house was filled with the fragrance of the perfume." When we truly waste ourselves on Jesus, whether it is by spending time with others, by spending time with Him on our own or by caring for the poor, something invisible and indescribable will fill the air; something wonderful will happen.

> True worship is to be so personally and hopelessly in love with God that the idea of a transfer of affection never even remotely exists.[2]

—A. W. Tozer

Notes

1. Matt Redman, "The Heart of Worship," © 1999 Kingsway's Thankyou Music.
2. A. W. Tozer, *Whatever Happened to Worship?* (Camp Hill, PA: Christian Publications, 1985), n.p.

Chapter 3

TEA, TOAST AND TORTOISES
(A chapter about prayer)

Let's face the facts: We're not very good at prayer. Sin, now that's a different story; we seem to be doing fairly well there—but prayer, well, ever since the disciples slumbered in the garden of Gethsemane, it seems like it's got us well and truly beaten. Or has it? Lately, God has been rousing the Church with a desire to tune in to the things that set His heart on fire and to pray accordingly. Strip away the kneeling and the old English language and prayer is basically communication with God. There are many types of prayer: confession, adoration, thanksgiving, and so forth. In this chapter, we are going to look at one aspect of prayer: asking. This is known in the trade as intercession, and it is exactly what people have been redis-covering lately. It's a world away from my early attempts at prayer, which always ended up with me dribbling onto my sleeve as I fell into a deep, deep sleep.

But whatever the style of prayer we're focusing on, we Christians find it to be one of the easiest things to get on a guilt trip about. How many times have we bought the line "God couldn't use you; you don't pray enough"? Like all good lies, it's based on a little truth. After all, how much is enough? Two hours out of 24 doesn't sound like much at all—but the thought of a four-hour quiet time would send most of us into a deep panic. The truth is that we need to learn to relax a little and know that life can be a prayer, and we need to learn to spend time communicating with our Father in heaven. However, while it is possible to communicate with someone who you love without saying anything, there comes a time when there's nothing left to do but to have a good chat. Instead of making prayer and intercession a legalistic "you ought to say your prayers, you ought to have your quiet time," it is helpful to get back to basics and find out exactly what it is that drives us to pray.

In Luke 11:1-10, Jesus described four steps to a solid prayer life:

One day Jesus was praying in a certain place. When he finished, one of his disciples said to Him, "Lord, teach us to pray, just as John taught his disciples." He said to them, "When you pray, say: 'Father, hallowed be your name, your kingdom come. Give us each day our daily bread. Forgive us our sins, for we also forgive everyone who sins against us. And lead us not into temptation.'" Then he said to them, "Suppose one of you has a friend, and he goes to him at midnight and says, 'Friend, lend me three loaves of bread, because a friend of mine on a journey has come to me, and I have nothing to set before him.'

Then the one inside answers, 'Don't bother me. The door is already locked, and my children are with me in bed. I can't get up and give you anything.' I tell you, though he will not get up and give him the bread because he is his friend, yet because of the man's boldness he will get up and give him as much as he needs. So I say to you: 'Ask and it will be given to you; seek and you will find; knock and the door will be opened to you. For everyone who asks receives; he who seeks finds; and to him who knocks, the door will be opened.'"

1. The Need

Like all good detective novels, there are clues scattered all around the Bible. In the text quoted above, Jesus does some major hint dropping. The scenario of an out-of-town friend turning up shows four conditions for prayer, without which prayer is dull and lifeless. The host is in desperate need of a bit of food, so desperate that he wakes up his friend in the middle of the night. I wouldn't get up for anyone in the middle of the night unless it was really, really important and I loved them more than I love my bed (which is a lot). And so the host fulfils the first condition for prayer—he had a need.

2. Nothing to Give

The cupboard was bare; there was no sign of the necessary provisions. Realizing that he cannot come up with the goods himself, the host knows that he needs help from somewhere else. In order to understand prayer, we need to realize that our own intelligence, money, popularity or resources cannot meet the needs of the world, or even the specific needs of those around us.

3. I Know a God Who Can

The host knows that his neighbor has plenty of the necessary provisions. Do we believe that God has exactly what we need? If we do, then we'll get on our knees just like the man who went to his neighbor's door, and we will . . .

4. Keep On Asking

Luke 11:7-8 refers to the toast-hunter's boldness as the deciding factor in the neighbor getting out of bed. The footnote that accompanies the story suggests that the word "boldness" could also be described as "persistence." Clearly, it's so boldly persistent that it's verging on cheeky. However, when we start praying, we can sometimes feel as though God has tucked up in His bed and can't be bothered to answer. At those times we give up, thinking that it would be rude to keep on asking; but it is at those times more than any other that we need to do as we're told and keep on knocking on the door, determined to wake up the whole neighborhood if necessary.

Of course, this doesn't mean that we should think of God as a glorified caterer, turning up whenever we click our fingers. We need to believe that God wants us to pray and understand that God wants us to feel as passionately about things as He does.

God Speed

This brings us into a head-on conflict between the way that we like things to happen and the way that they actually do. We love lightning-quick answers to prayer. Occasionally they do happen, but most of the time these are a little on the rare side, leaving us frustrated and offended at God's apparent disinterest. The truth, according to Colin Urquhart, is that the Lord often answers in two ways: with the lightning response and with the tortoise response.[1] The lightning-quick response is exciting and immediate, but more often the Lord sends His answer tucked up in a shell: the tortoise response. Often, the little fellow has only managed to get half way when we get bored and give up all hope of ever receiving an answer. Knowing that we've given up, the tortoise turns round and goes home. While I'm not sure exactly how far we can take this metaphor (if God uses tortoises, what happens when they hibernate?), I reckon it's a good bit of encouragement to persevere in prayer.

> I have posted watchmen on your walls, O Jerusalem;
> they will never be silent day or night.
> You who call on the LORD give yourselves no rest,
> and give him no rest till he establishes Jerusalem
> and makes her the praise of the earth (Isa. 62:6-7).

This is another instruction from God to be persistent in prayer. He says that we must never give up until He answers.

Cheeky!

Another example of Biblical persistence is when God slipped Abraham His plans for a reshuffling of Sodom, a city that was constantly topping the Most Unrighteous City charts. Abraham's response was simple but effective; he challenged

God's plan. He went on to display bartering skills that any secondhand car dealer would be proud of and managed to convince God to save the city if He could find 10 righteous people in it. Through Abraham's reverent perseverance, he managed to influence God (see Genesis 18—19).

But does this mean that left on His own, God would make poor decisions? Do we have to watch His every move like a warden in a retirement home in case He sets fire to His dressing gown? Of course not. The truth is that God loves it when we get our prayer-fangs stuck into something, because that means we are developing our relationship with Him.

Surprise

This also provides the answer to one of those questions that always used to trip me up: What's the point in continually asking God to do something that He wants to do anyway? When we're interceding, God often does more than just answer our prayers: In getting closer to Him, we cannot fail to be changed. To put it another way, the tortoise often has a few surprises tucked in his shell.

In Ezekiel 4, we see that the prophet was on the receiving end of one or two of those surprises. There are certain passages of Scripture that you can become so familiar with that you actually forget what they are about. For me, the book of Ezekiel—the story of one of God's nuttiest prophets—is precisely one of those passages. As well as showing God's love for His people, it makes a potent statement about the value of prophetic intercession and shows Ezekiel going through all sorts of pain but ending up infinitely closer to God.

Ezekiel is told by God to "take a clay tablet, put it in front of you and draw the city of Jerusalem on it" (Ezek. 4:1). Ezekiel's next instruction is to "lay siege to it," to bring on his pretend soldiers and have himself a little war game (see v. 2). A little strange perhaps, but in the privacy of your own home this might not be too worrying. The trouble was that God wanted this particular display of prophetic toy soldiers to be a very public one.

As Ezekiel lay on his left side, he was giving the whole of Israel a sign: not that his grip on reality was flimsy, but that their grasp of disobedience was firm. Ezekiel lay on his side for 390 days, each day symbolizing a year of Israel's sin. He then lay on his right side for 40 days, each day representing a year of the sin of the house of Judah. For over 14 months, Ezekiel laid in front of his reconstruction of Israel, tied up with ropes and eating no more than 200 grams of unleavened bread per day.

At the end of it all, God told Ezekiel to stand up and, "with bared arm," prophesy to Israel (Ezek. 4:7). Ezekiel's naked arm would not have been a pretty sight after a year of being squashed by his body (can you imagine the bed sores?). As Ezekiel lifted his arm to speak to Israel, he would have felt something of the pain that God would have felt for the 390 years of Israel's sin. Ezekiel's physical and mental state would have meant that his words would not have been packaged with the polite niceties that we often hear today ("Excuse me, Israel, but you've been a bit naughty now, haven't you?" would not have been his opening phrase). As he spat out the words, he felt the absolute pain of the torture he had endured and touched a part of God's heart that had suffered the same. Ezekiel's story gives us a clear job description for the prophetic intercessor: to feel God's pain. That is why we often end up weeping when we pray.

The Christmas List Crisis

As a slightly younger human being, I suffered a yearly dose of anxiety each time the Christmas decorations went up. Should I make a list or simply enjoy the surprises? A list, you may think, would be the obvious choice; but being a particularly innocent "young pup," I was especially vulnerable when it came to the latest *big thing*. Whatever I was willing to lose a limb for in November, I would be desperately trying to dismantle in December. I spent many a Christmas day devising devious plans to sell my brand-new boxed item in order to upgrade it to the vastly superior version that I had seen only the day before. My parents' choices were little better, and if I had taken the option marked "surprise" every year, I would have ended up with enough junior chemistry sets to run a hospital. Things are a little calmer now, but every once in a while, I go through a similar crisis about prayer. Are my constant requests to God any better than my childhood desires for the newest, biggest and best? After all, just what should we be praying for? Is it even right to keep on asking God for all these things?

Back to basics, God likes us to pray and to believe that He will answer. In one conversation with His disciples, Jesus says the following:

And I will do whatever you ask in my name, so that the Son may bring glory to the Father. You may ask me for anything in my name, and I will do it (John 14:13-14).

If you remain in me and my words remain in you, ask whatever you wish, and it will be given you (John 15:7).

You did not choose me, but I chose you and appointed you to go and bear fruit—fruit that will last. Then the Father will give you whatever you ask in my name (John 15:16).

Until now you have not asked for anything in my name. Ask and you will receive, and your joy will be complete (John 16:24).

Do you think Jesus was trying to tell them something? Unfortunately, this doesn't quite give us a blank check with which to go out and bag a Porsche or win the lottery, so what are the boundaries? John 15:7 gives us the clue: "If you remain in me and my words remain in you, ask whatever you wish, and it will be given you." This seems to be a good verse for intercessors. Spending time with God, remaining in Him and depending on Him like a branch on a vine will get us closer to Him and closer to His heart. The closer we are to God's heart, the more likely we are to be in tune with what He wants. Avoiding the Christmas list crisis and spending time with God are sure ways to be asking for the right things.

"So do I have to give up what I'm doing now and lie on my side for the next year?" Good point. Most of us would find it hard to be a full-time player in the Ezekiel league of prophetic intercession, but does that mean that our prayer lives are nonstarters? Certainly not, for though there will be some who are made for that side of things, to whom perhaps those stories really speak, most of us will find a slightly less intense rhythm of prayer. Returning to the beginning of this chapter, prayer starts when we see a need, realize that we cannot sort it out ourselves, and believe that God can help. This applies both to the fall of a nation and the pain of a friend. God cares about both and hears the prayers with equal compassion.

But what if we lack the time or the energy to intercede for hours on end? Is it an all-or-nothing situation in which if we don't lock ourselves away for 12 hours a day we might as well not bother at all? I hope not. Perhaps we see prayer in too narrow terms. I think there is a place for knuckling down and concentrating on speaking to the Lord, but spending time chatting with Him is equally valid. There's a place for taking a walk, talking to the Lord with the backdrop of His creation.

Often I'll pray in tongues in all sorts of locations, and I believe that this is a powerful way of spending time with God. I remember when I first heard of this bizarre, magical gift that only a few ever receive. At first, I thought that speaking in tongues was a like a Knighthood; it was only given if you were part of the in-crowd, but pretty useless when you had it. Still, I fancied getting me some, so I asked a couple of friends in the church to give it to me. They soon straightened me out, suggesting that I ask God to give it to me instead. The plan was pretty simple (almost too simple, I thought, but I didn't want to burst their bubble). We would ask God to give me the gift of tongues, and then they would start to speak in tongues themselves. After a while one of them would then touch my lips and I would say the first thing that came to my mouth.

I began to get nervous once we reached the lip touching stage. Until then, I had simply been enjoying the beautiful sound of my friends' strange language, but now I realized that I would have to pull something pretty impressive out of the bag if I wasn't going to disappoint. I had my hands outstretched and my eyes shut, but I could feel them willing me on. There was no point in delaying, so I went for it.

"Shalla Balla," I said, and then stood up to get my coat.

"Oh thank you, Lord," said one friend.

"Yes, thank you for giving Mike the gift of tongues," said the other.

They both wore smiles that matched their words and seemed genuinely convinced that I was the recipient of a *spiritual gift* and not *verbal vomiting*. So I gave it another try:

"SHALLA BALLA, *BEELA* BALLA."

This made my friends even more excited, so I pitched in with a few more words. After an hour or so, we stopped to chat. They understood my surprise that it all seemed so simple and told me that it was just about another way of praying when we don't quite know what to pray. They suggested that I spend 10 minutes doing it each day, learning to communicate with God. It made such a difference in my relationship that I have stuck with it ever since.

In the New Testament, we see many people speaking in tongues, using it as a prayer language. There are many times when we are stuck for knowing how or what to pray, or even how to express our love for God. The gift of tongues is the Holy Spirit praying within us. When we start, it can sound like baby-talk, as it did with me, but I eventually found out that the secret is not to concentrate on what is being said, but to focus on Jesus. I have found it to be one of the greatest helps imaginable to my prayer life.

Another way is to pray the Scriptures. Why not take a psalm or one of the great prayers of the Bible and then read them out as your prayer to God? Thankfully, we are all different, and what might be helpful for one person may be a waste of time for another. The important thing to remember is that we all need to find the ways of praying that work for us. Whatever the situation, it is always possible to pause and take a little time out with God, which after all, is a pretty good way of getting closer to Him and understanding what He wants for our lives.

Note

1. Colin Urquhart, *Anything You Ask* (London: Hodder and Stoughton, 2001), n.p.

Chapter 4

GOD WHISPERS TO HIS FRIENDS
(A chapter about listening to God)

When you hear the word "prophecy," what do you think? Do you think about strange people with big hair and peculiar diets? Do you think about messages that start out "I'm getting a picture of a sheep . . ."?

The truth is that prophecy is one of the aspects of the Christian life that we seem to misunderstand or forget about altogether. Whether we dismiss it because we think it's mystical or because we think it's mundane, we run the risk of missing out on hearing God's voice and receiving His direction. To take it back to basics, we believe in a God who speaks. He has always spoken to His people, and He speaks to us today. For many of us, the biggest problem is knowing how to hear Him and how to recognize His voice—and boy do we need to hear the voice of God today.

I used to think that prophecy was limited to certain meetings. You know the ones: a circle of chairs in a church hall where after a while someone gets up and says, "I have a picture of a waterfall/lake/river." There's nothing wrong with this, but it wasn't until a few years ago that I realized that biblical prophecy, the sort that we see throughout the Scriptures, is totally relevant to every aspect of our lives today. It's about God talking to us. It's about the Church becoming people led not by good ideas but by His voice and Spirit.

Doing My Part for the European Union

A while back, I spent three years as youth pastor at Saint Andrew's Chorleywood, an Anglican church just outside London. When I had finished, my boss, Bishop David Pytches, found me another job in the church, and I didn't think twice about it until the day came when I actually stopped being the youth worker and the new person started. With his arrival came the thought, *What have I done? They're my young people; they belong to me and now he's got them.* I remember the first Friday the youth met with him: I sat in my home, praying and trying to be holy, asking the Lord to bless my (ex) youth group with their new leader. I stopped praying pretty quickly. The whole thing hurt, and to my surprise, I went through a real bereavement process. For the next six months I grieved and missed them terribly, all of which was made worse by the fact that I didn't feel settled or fulfilled in my new job. I started to think about leaving.

Then I went to France with a friend who also worked at the church. Barry and I were going to do a youth conference, and as we were driving, I told Barry how I felt. When we arrived, we met up with the local pastors to have a meal and talk about the conference. We hadn't met before, so they knew nothing about me, and at the end of the meal we decided to pray. In the middle of the prayer time, one of the pastors got up and walked away from the table. He went to the coat stand, picked up a little girl's duffle coat, and then walked back and stood in front of me. Holding the coat open, he spoke.

"Put the coat on," he said.

Oh dear, I thought. I shrugged a silent reply that said "I can't" and hoped that he might go and ask someone else to join in his little game.

"Put the coat on," he repeated.

"I can't," I said. Desperately in need of support, I looked at Barry, who looked down and closed his eyes. Again the demented pastor with poor vision asked me to put it on. In the hope of avoiding an international incident, I tried to put my fingers in the sleeve.

"I can't," I said as I tried to get my hand out again.

"Why not?"

Now I knew what I was dealing with. Slowly, pronouncing every syllable as if my entire reputation depended upon it, I replied, "Because it does not fit."

"Exactly," came his reply. "And God says to you, 'Stop running back and trying to put on the old coat. It doesn't fit you anymore.' Let God give you the new coat, the new ministry. You're feeling naked because you're between ministries. Don't run back to the thing that's safe; let God give you the new coat. Put the new ministry on."

Suddenly, I was shaken by the realization that God really does exist—and that He knows about me. It didn't make everything perfect, but I knew that God knew me and that He had a plan for me. It was so right for me at the time, and I had never encountered anything like it before. This pastor was willing to take a risk and God spoke profoundly through it, just like we see in Scripture.

Hungry for More

I returned home desperate to hear God speak as powerfully as He had through the French pastor. I started reading passages of Scripture in a new way. One of these passages was 1 Corinthians 14:1, which states, "Follow the way of love and eagerly desire spiritual gifts, especially the gift of prophesy."

This means that we are to be keen to get our hands on those spiritual gifts like nothing else. Until the penny dropped, I had been pretty cool about receiving these gifts. "O Lord," I had prayed, "I will not seek after the gifts; I am simply happy with the giver." I thought I was being spiritual and holy, but it was a pretty false and unbiblical spirituality. In not wanting to be a "gift junky" and ignoring God's gifts, I was ignoring God, missing out on the chance to get a lot closer to Him. Reading what Paul wrote to the church at Corinth, it is clear that "eagerly desir[ing] . . . especially the gift of prophecy" is not about being self-indulgent; it is about being strengthened, encouraged and comforted (see 1 Cor. 14:3). This is the purpose of New Testament prophecy.

Prophecy is not meant to be a substitute for the Word of God; we must never lose the study of the Book in favor of the Lord's giving us a quick prophecy instead of a quiet time. Reading the Bible is by far the best way to hear God and to learn more about His character. Maybe we don't see so much of God waving little duffle coats around in the Bible, but we do see Him giving encouragement and guidance to His children. Throughout the book of Acts, there are tons of instances where the apostles recognized God's voice and put His commands into action as they established the Early Church. Prophecy today is as relevant as it was then.

For a while after I returned from France, I asked the Lord to teach me about hearing Him speak; then I met a vicar named Bruce Collins. We were both involved in a retreat for church leaders that was run by Saint Andrew's, and every six weeks or so, on the last night of each course, Bruce would come and pray for each person and ask God to speak. I heard about this and asked if I could go along. Everyone took turns being prayed for by Bruce and a member of his team while all the others sat around and prayed. I found what I saw and heard hard to believe; each time, Bruce or someone from his team spoke prophetic words that were incredibly accurate and helpful. Everybody seemed to be strengthened and encouraged and comforted when God spoke. I knew that I was seeing people's lives being changed for good right in front of me.

I ran through a little checklist in my head to see if I thought the words were from God. Did each prophetic word line up with Scripture? Were the people left strengthened, encouraged and comforted as a result? Did it lead people to Jesus? When the Lord spoke to me in France, my response wasn't "Oh, isn't this French pastor wonderful," but it was to worship Jesus. Revelation 19:10 says that "the testimony of Jesus is the spirit of prophecy."

At the end of the first meeting, I told Bruce how much I wanted to be able to hear God. I think I was feeling a bit annoyed because I'd tried so hard since I had returned from France to find the gift of prophecy, but all I had managed to get was the *gift of frustration.* I had tried so hard to tune in and *be prophetic,* but all that I came up with was the word "spaghetti." There's nothing wrong with the word, but there's only so much you can do with it: "You're worried about your job? God says that it is like spaghetti." "You've got too much on your plate." or "You think you might be pregnant? God says, 'spaghetti.' It's quite good for you." I told Bruce about this and he said I needed to practice listening to God and that I could come along to help at the next prophecy night.

Embarrassment

Because it was six weeks away, I agreed to do it. I had originally intended to pray and fast until the meeting so that I might be spiritually prepared, but it didn't seem to happen. I completely forgot until the day came when I was supposed to sit next to Bruce and prophesy to these 16 church leaders and their spouses. That afternoon, I prayed that I would be sick; I prayed that they would be sick; I prayed for the Second

Coming. At 7:30 P.M., I went along and sat next to Bruce while he explained a little bit about how God speaks. I was working on Plan B, getting my reserve words ready ("The Lord says, 'You're a woman'"), but I knew I'd get caught up. So I began to bargain: *Please, Lord, give me a prophecy just this once. I'll pray every day for the rest of my life. I'll be a missionary.*

The first couple came forward and we started to pray. By this time I was getting frantic, hearing a mixture of silence and total internal panic. But then, ever so faintly I began to hear a song. Could this be a prophetic song, speaking truth and power in a beautiful tongue? I strained to work out what it was, getting ready to deliver, and then it hit me: ABBA, "Dancing Queen." *Leave it out, Lord, give me something sensible* was my most spiritual reaction. Bruce had pretty much finished giving his words, and I knew I didn't have much time. He (along with everyone else) turned to me.

"And, Mike, what do you have?"

I smiled, closed my eyes and prayed, *Lord, you've got five seconds.* When it was clear that there was nothing other than the Swedish Pop-combo's Greatest Dancehall Classic in my head, I knew I had to say it. I took a good look at this vicar's wife and got ready to throw my entire (but small) reputation out the window.

"I think the Lord would say to you, in the words of ABBA, 'you can dance, you can jive, having the time of your life.'" And then I wanted to die.

The lady started to laugh. *Thanks very much*, I thought. *If ever I meet you and you make a fool of yourself, I hope I'm there to have a good giggle too.*

"I suppose you're wondering why we're laughing," she said when she had calmed down a little.

No, I thought.

"Three weeks ago, I started a dance group in my church with two other women. As we were coming to this meeting, I said to my husband—didn't I, dear—what am I doing starting a dance group? I shouldn't be doing something like that; I can't dance."

Numbers 12:6-8 seems to explain the whole ABBA thing. Aaron and Miriam were complaining to God about Moses, when they were given this reply:

> When a prophet of the LORD is among you,
> I reveal myself to him in visions,
> I speak to him in dreams.
> But this is not true of my servant Moses . . .
> With him I speak face to face,
> clearly and not in riddles;
> he sees the form of the LORD.
> Why then were you not afraid
> to speak against my servant Moses?

If you think about it, God says that apart from Moses, He speaks to the rest of His prophets in visions, dreams and riddles. He does not speak clearly. This means that spending a life listening to God speak could very well include a whole lot more ABBA incidents. Great!

Whispers from God

So why does God speak like this? Besides the obvious benefit of keeping people like me firmly in their place, I suspect that one reason is to stretch our faith. The Scriptures say that we prophesy according to our faith (see Rom. 12:6). If God spoke to us prophetically by bellowing, "Hear ye, hear ye, God calling Mike. Are you receiving me?" there would be little place for faith or for taking a risk and choosing to believe in God. Perhaps another reason is that God is more interested in relationship with us than in anything else. It's fair to say that in Scripture, God shouts to His enemies and whispers to His friends. Jesus said to His disciples, "The knowledge of the secrets of the kingdom of heaven has been given to you" (Matt. 13:11). He revealed those secrets with whispering parables, examples and actions; things that started the disciples thinking, things that drew them close to Him.

I was at my sister's house a few years ago when my six-year-old niece walked into the room. "Jo, come here. Mommy wants to tell you something," said my sister, and Jo, being six, said, "No."

"Come here. Mommy's got a secret to tell you."

"What's the secret?" asked Jo.

"If mommy told you from here to there it wouldn't be a secret, because everyone else in the room would hear."

Getting a little excited, Jo said, "Tell me now," and moved a few paces closer.

"The secret's this . . ."

"What?" Jo said.

"You'll have to come closer." Jo came closer . . . and then it was too late. My sister grabbed hold of her and said, "The secret's this—mommy loves you!" and kissed her.

Afterwards, I thought that sometimes God whispers to us to make us get so close that we really listen to Him. No one has a special hotline to God; it's just a matter of responding to Him when He asks us to get closer. I used to repent before I saw Bruce; I thought that if he looked into my eyes, he would see all my sin. Thankfully, that is not the way it works; God wants us to get closer to Him so that we can be strengthened, encouraged and comforted—not so that we can get the dirt on our friends.

More Embarrassments

Later that year, we were having another prophecy meeting with visiting clergy. I remember meeting one couple and the wife said to me, "Hello, you're Greek aren't you?"

"Yes, I am," I replied. She then told me that she had lived in Athens for a while.

As we were praying for her, a Greek swear word came into my mind. Trying not to look embarrassed, I started thinking about something else, but it was no good. The word was *skadula*, which means "female excrement." As we were praying, I thought, *What's the point? If she doesn't know the word it won't mean anything, and if she does she'll smack me!* Bruce then chipped in, "Mike, I think God's given you something."

I tried to use some common sense, so phrasing my question carefully I asked her, "When you lived in Greece, did people say bad words to you?" Straight away tears came into her eyes and she said yes. I said, "The Lord wants to say to you that in His eyes you are not a skadula."

I couldn't believe the response. She sobbed and sobbed. She had lived in Greece and had married a Greek man who had abused her and given her the nickname "skadula." He used to introduce her to his friends as "my skadula." God broke through and started to heal her in an amazing way. That's how it works.

There are plenty of people who could tell better stories about how God has worked in the prophetic, but the point is that it is important to remember that this gift is for all of us. We need to eagerly desire the spiritual gifts, especially that we might prophesy, and we need to take the word seriously. As we do it He will speak to us, and in faith we will begin to speak words. Sometimes we will get it wrong. This is the way we learn to tell what comes from God and what comes from our own imagination.

And Another Embarrassment

Even though I would much rather you get it wrong for yourselves, I suppose I had better let you know about one of my best/worst times ever. When I was beginning to learn about prophecy, I went to the Isle of Man to speak at some meetings. In the first meeting, we prayed for some words and got some that seemed to be fairly accurate. The congregation had never experienced this before, and they seemed very encouraged by it. So we kept on and spent quite a bit of time on this during the week, during which God was really good to all of us.

Before the final meeting, at which about 300 people from different parts of the island came, I was sitting on the toilet, minding my own business. A couple of guys were outside my cubicle, unaware of the fact that I was in there. One guy said to the other, "Oh, I can't wait for tonight. That Mike Pilavachi is so amazing; he's such a Prophet. God's going to give him some awesome words tonight." I sat there with a satisfied smile on my face and told the Lord that we were going to have a great meeting.

After the worship I strode in, accompanied by my *prophetic look*. I spent a few minutes strolling up and down, staring at people and twitching my eyebrows. I looked good! Suddenly I stopped when I saw a woman, and the phrase "Put on your dancing shoes" came into my mind. It seemed to be a good one, so I gave it a go.

"That lady there, would you stand? God is about to speak to you," I announced in my deepest, most prophetic voice. "The Lord would say unto you 'Put on your dancing shoes.'" I looked around as everyone was waiting in rapt attention. "Would you like to share how you've been blessed by that word?"

She stood there in silence for some time, looking a bit awkward. I decided to help her with the interpretation.

"Do you dance?"

"Not really," she said.

"Aah! You don't dance," I replied, confident that this would be the launch of one of the most powerful dancing careers of the century.

"Yes, I do, sometimes alone in the room. Not too much, not too little."

I tried hard to find a spiritual significance, and then I remembered that passage from Psalms that says, "You have turned for me my mourning into dancing" (Ps. 30:11, *NKJV*). I decided that this must be it, so I said, "Perhaps you're in mourning? Has someone close to you died?"

She paused. "I don't think so. A woman down the road died six months ago, but I hardly knew her."

There followed one of the most embarrassing moments of my life as this woman and I tried every way to make the word fit. Eventually I realized what was going on and I had to face up and say to everyone, "Sorry, folks, I got that one wrong." I've had a lot of "good" times like that.

If you are looking for a reason why this happens, the answer is one of the clearest that you can find in Scripture. There's a passage that's repeated three times, which is very rare for the Bible. The verse can be found in Proverbs, in the book of James and in the first letter of Peter: "God opposes the proud and gives grace to the humble" (Jas. 4:6; 1 Pet. 5:5; see Prov. 3:34), and God repeats it because He means it. Since that is the truth, I vote for humbling myself from now on; it's a lot less painful. We will get it wrong, so let's not pretend. Anyway, prophecy is more about us getting closer to God than it is about us climbing higher than our friends.

Often we don't expect to hear, so we don't listen or jot things down. Put this book down and begin to listen to the Lord. You don't need to go up to people and say, "The Lord told me," "The Lord says" or "I know your secret sin." Sometimes offering to pray for the person next to you in church is the best way to say what you believe God is saying to you. We will all fail as we develop the gift of prophecy, but as we do, keep in mind a basic truth: There is no need to super-spiritualize things. God whispers to us, His friends, not because He fancies a laugh or wants to make us look good, but because He loves us and wants us close to Him.

Part 2:
GETTING STEADY

Chapter 5

WALKING THE TIGHTROPE
(This one's about faith)

Faith—you can lose it, gain it, share it and heal with it. To some people, just having it will send you to the right place when your body is six feet under; to others, it is enough to kill for. Some talk of good and bad faith; others talk listlessly of not having it, as if it were similar to a heated towel. Face the facts—faith is confusing, and with so many opinions going around it can be kind of hard to sort out. Let's start at first base then . . .

What Is Faith?

Whatever faith is, the Bible is full of it. More than that, it seems that Jesus got really excited about it too. For example, when the centurion said to Jesus, "Lord, I do not deserve to have you come under my roof. But say the word, and my servant will be healed" (Matt. 8:8), Jesus left him with a five-star endorsement: "I have not found anyone in Israel with such great faith" (Matt. 8:10), He said. At other times Jesus healed the sick and added "Because of your faith you've been made well" (see Matt. 9:29; Mark 10:51; Luke 17:19). He loved to see faith in people.

God not only loves faith, but faith also brings Him pleasure. Hebrews 11:6 pulls no punches with the line "And without faith it is impossible to please God." Anyone who comes to God must believe that He exists and that He rewards those who earnestly seek Him. That is a potentially depressing thought, and I have heard more than a few people say, "I wish I could believe, but I just don't have the faith." To many, faith is an unscalable object that is best left alone. Thankfully that does not have to be the case, and God loves to tickle our hearts and get us interested, but sooner or later it's time to sign on the dotted line.

Is Faith Something That You Think?

To an extent, our Christian faith is based on concrete evidence. Part of the success of the Alpha course (an 11-week course in practical Christian faith that began at Trinity Brompton Church in London) has come from its commitment to exploring the facts of Christianity (How do we know Christ lived? How do we know that Christianity is for real?). Knowing the facts of Christianity is vital to faith, especially at times when nothing feels right.

Is Faith Something That You Feel?

This too is correct. There may have been times in your life when you have felt that God is real, when it all seems to make sense and life is great. Chances are if you've experienced this, then you've touched the other side of the coin: the place where nothing is real, nothing works and nothing exists. Unfortunately, feelings are unreliable, but still, they should not be sniffed at. It's great when you sincerely believe that God is going to do something, but those times cannot be relied on to be there every time we call on God. The sort of faith that we see throughout the Bible is a little more than something that you think or feel. One of the biggest clues available can be found in Mark 2.

A few days later, when Jesus again entered Capernaum, the people heard that he had come home. So many gathered that there was no room left, not even outside the door, and he preached the word to them. Some men came, bringing to him a paralytic, carried by four of them. Since they could not get him to Jesus because of the crowd, they made an opening in the roof above Jesus and, after digging through it, lowered the mat the paralyzed man was lying on. When Jesus saw their faith, he said to the paralytic, "Son, your sins are forgiven."

Now some teachers of the law were sitting there, thinking to themselves, "Why does this fellow talk like that? He's blaspheming! Who can forgive sins but God alone?"

Immediately Jesus knew in his spirit that this was what they were thinking in their hearts, and he said to them,

"Why are you thinking these things? Which is easier: to say
to the paralytic, 'Your sins are forgiven,' or to say, 'Get up,
take your mat and walk'? But that you may know that the
Son of Man has authority on earth to forgive sins . . ."
He said to the paralytic, "I tell you, get up, take your mat
and go home" (Mark 2:1-11).

This story always amazes me. Think about it carefully
and it becomes clear that the bizarre nature of the encounter
carries an equally powerful message. In Matthew's version of
the story, the house in question was owned by a Levite, so
this was an audience with some of the more respected members of society. As they sat there, politely listening to the
man they couldn't quite understand, little did they know
that a bunch of guys were about to ruin the whole meeting
and get blessed by the Son of God for their trouble. What
starts out with a little dust in the air soon ends up with the
ceiling falling on their heads and a paralytic man being lowered down on a mat.

Now, they took a huge risk there; can you imagine if it
hadn't worked out? The owner of the house would have been
totally justified in beating their heads in. Imagine his embar-
rassment as societies' elite gathered in his front room only to
be subjected to a bizarre terrorist healing attack. Thankfully,
Jesus' reaction was a little less predictable: When He saw
their faith, He said to the man, "Your sins are forgiven . . .
get up take your mat and walk." What does it mean when it
says "Jesus saw their faith"? Did He see faith written on
their foreheads? Did He see a look of faith on their faces?

What is an expression of faith anyway? How do you get one? I think what Jesus saw was a hole in the roof. He saw what their faith had inspired them to do: an act of incredible foolishness inspired by their belief that Jesus could help them.

The stories of Jesus' time on Earth are littered with similar examples of people who have believed in Him and acted on their belief. The centurion believed so strongly that Jesus would heal his servant that he didn't even need Jesus to visit. There was the woman who was hemorrhaging blood who touched Jesus' cloak expecting something to happen (see Mark 5:25-34). Peter and John said to the paralyzed man at the gate Beautiful in Acts 3:6, "In the name of Jesus Christ of Nazareth, walk." What they all have in common is faith, but not just faith as a feeling, or even as a thought: In each case, it is a motivator that initiates action. As I learned at school, a verb is a doing word: "faith" is a verb.

Genesis 12 to 22 describe Abraham as being a believer in God whose faith was credited to him as righteousness. In other words, the way that he lived his life, acting on the belief that God was almighty God, made God extremely happy. Because Abraham believed in God, he left his home for a place in which he was a stranger; because he believed in God, he believed that he would have a son. Thankfully (for us), this doesn't mean that Abraham lived a supercharged, problem-free life; sleeping with Hagar could be seen as a "low point," for example. However, he maintained his belief in God, making bold decisions and brave sacrifices because of that belief. In Abraham's case, the presence of faith did not mean the absence of doubt.

Having been a youth worker, I am always keen to keep up with the "kidz." Recently, I was on an online search engine, when I decided to search for someone I had heard of called *Blondin*, who made his name as an incredibly gifted tightrope walker. I ended up at two websites: first at *Encyclopaedia Britannica* and second at one that told people how to become a Christian. Here's what I read:

Blondin: (Born Feb. 28, 1824, Saint-Omer, France—died Feb. 19, 1897, Little Ealing, near London, England) Pseudonym of JEAN-FRANCOIS GRAVELET, tightrope walker and acrobat who owed his celebrity and fortune to his feat of crossing Niagara Falls on a tightrope 1,100 feet long, 160 feet above the water.[1]

It's about faith: Blondin, the famous French tightrope walker, strung a cable across the Niagara Falls. There's a huge crowd watching. And as they watch, he walks across and all the way back. Like he was out for a Sunday stroll.

The crowd goes wild. He says to them, "Do you believe that I could walk across to the other side with this wheelbarrow?" And they all cheer and scream and say, "Yeah! We believe that you can walk across there with a wheelbarrow." No problem. They've seen him walk it easily. It shouldn't be too much harder. They believed he could do it.

Blondin then says, "Okay, you believe I can do it. You've seen me walk across there. Who's going to get in the wheelbarrow and come with me?"

And there was a deathly hush. See, it's a different thing altogether, isn't it? You can believe that he can do it. But when it comes to believing in him, there's an element of personal commitment being called for.[2]

Now, I'm not going to go on some trip about how the *Encyclopaedia Britannica* is missing the point, but I do think that the second section is far more revealing than the first. Those people who watched, applauded and refused to get in the wheelbarrow exercised a shallow faith that gave in to their fears for their own lives. That is not the sort of faith that we see exhibited in the Bible; instead, we see countless examples of people who are willing to believe in God in spite of worries about themselves.

Face it, though, most of us wouldn't trust Blondin to give us a ride over Niagara Falls, and similarly most of us get a little shy when we feel one of those "divine opportunities" coming our way. Our reaction is nothing new: When writing to the Early Church, James pointed out, "You believe that there is one God. Good! Even the demons believe that—and shudder" (Jas. 2:19). There is a long line of people who "Believe in God," but the one that really matters is the line marked " . . . And Are Prepared to Do Something About It." The praise of the spectators 160 feet below meant nothing to Blondin when they refused to trust him. The praise of God is worthless if we are not prepared to hop into His wheelbarrow.

How Do You Get Faith?

Method One: Ask. As the father of the demon-possessed boy in Mark 9:24 said, "I believe; help me overcome my unbelief!"

Faith is a gift, and like all gifts we shouldn't feel bad about asking God for it. As we have already seen, faith is one of those gifts that is a response to Him, and God, being who He is, may well respond to a request for help with a chance to practice. I remember once hearing someone give the "I want to believe, but I just don't have the faith" line. Days later, that person heard the gospel; something clicked and before he knew it, he was faced with a chance to use faith. This does not happen to everyone, which is why when some people hear the gospel it leaves them cold.

Method Two: Through the Word. Romans 10:17 explains that faith comes by hearing and hearing by the Word of God. At times, just hearing the gospel preached can fire people up with faith to commit their lives. It seems that the Church is beginning to rediscover how to preach the gospel through works and deeds (a pivotal part of our faith), but it is important that we do not reject proclaiming the gospel through words. Like many aspects of our faith, the secret is in the balance. As Paul understood, there is a power in the gospel and a power in proclaiming Jesus.

There is a second part to the connection between faith and the Word and it applies perhaps more to those who have already made a commitment. The Bible is full of inspirational and interactive stuff. At times, a passage written by someone else that seems to describe our situation exactly will excite us. At other times, the stories of other people are like dynamite. When I read the stories of God's faithfulness to Abraham, Moses and David, I am inspired. I think, *I want to be like that. I want my life to be like that.* When I read the acts of the apostles and I see the faith of the first Christians, I think, *Wow, this is the same God*. Because we're bombarded all our lives with things that would undermine our faith, it is so important that we read the Word. Here in front of us is the last word in practical advice.

The Opposition to Faith

Faith is all about our response to God, and our own personal faith will be as individual and unique as the very character of the Creator. We all have been through our own experiences, doubts, insecurities and pains, and these will make for our own stumbling blocks. My faith will be different from your faith, just as my pain is different from yours. However, the wisdom of God is available to us, and through it we can understand ourselves a little better and learn to deal with these stumbling blocks.

A childhood full of disappointments will inevitably change you. As early promises of toys and treats are made, they are believed in with an innocence and faith. A few broken promises down the line and the response changes to "Yeah, I'll take that with a pinch of salt." The pain of the early disappointments teaches a new reaction, one that means we don't get hurt. Perhaps it is not surprising that we can carry these attitudes over from our childhood into our relationship with God, suspiciously eyeing up His promises. But as with all living things, our healing takes time, and our emotions are especially fragile. For God to be a living force in our lives, He needs us to respond to Him. Through the stories and examples of His character that we find in the Bible, we can begin to trust Him and begin to see that His promises are solid and for real, unlike those thrown at us like sweets to quiet us down.

When I became a Christian, there was an illustration of a train that everybody seemed to use. The engine was called *Facts*, the first carriage *Faith* and the second *Feelings*. For the whole thing to work, the engine had to be in front, pulling the carriages. If our faith is following the facts, then the feelings will follow behind. If we decide to put our feelings up front, then the train goes nowhere. The 1970s were full of things like that.

Maybe you find it hard to believe that when you've confessed your sins, God has forgiven you. Despite your prayers you feel dirty, unclean and guilty. If you choose (and sometimes it is a difficult choice to make) to put your faith in your feelings, then you'll believe that you aren't forgiven. But if you decide to look at the facts and see in Scripture that Jesus died for all men and women, that His blood is sufficient to cover all sin, then you will find it a lot easier to believe that you are forgiven. It may take a while, but the feelings will follow. This can happen in any situation, although I'm not saying that it is easy. But as Jesus said, "You will know the truth, and the truth will set you free" (John 8:32).

How Do We Grow in Faith?

As with much of the Christian life, there seems to be a lot of false propaganda going around. Faith comes in for more than its fair share as we are frequently confronted with the assumption that having true faith means never having any doubts. As I've heard John Wimber say, "Faith is spelled R-I-S-K." If we are not prepared to risk failure, we will find it hard to develop our faith. If you are about to risk your whole reputation, career or life, you would have to be a robot not to think twice; you are bound to have doubts. Deciding to do something for the first time, stepping out of the comfort zone and saying "Either God's going to come, or I've had it" is a scary place to be, but there's no better place. Some of us never hop into the wheelbarrow, and so faith remains malnourished and underdeveloped. Thankfully, help is at hand, and all we need to do is say yes. To grow in faith is to begin to live like that, and the more you do it the more you grow.

Faith is important to the whole of our lives. Even prophecy is linked to faith, as it says in Scripture that we prophesy according to our faith (see Rom. 12:6). In fact, you can swap the word "prophecy" here for all sorts of things: We love according to our faith. We are vulnerable according to our faith. We forgive according to our faith. We see miracles happen according to our faith. We venture out and do great exploits according to our faith. Returning to Hebrews 11, we read that "by faith" all manner of biblical exploits were carried out. We too will grow in faith by stepping out in faith; like muscles, the more we exercise our faith, the more it grows. However, that doesn't mean that it ever gets easy, because, unlike for muscles, there are no steroids for faith.

Practically, we have found much of this out at Soul Survivor. The first time we ever put on a festival, we were gripped by the fear of two simple questions: Will anyone come? and Will we go bankrupt? (In case you're wondering, the answers were yes and not quite.) We had doubts right from the start, but did that mean we lacked faith? The mark of that would have been if we had called it off. Obviously, faith has to be a response to God's Word, and with the festival we believed that God had told us to do it. A few years later, we bought a warehouse for our local church in Watford. The building cost £300,000 (approximately U.S. $530,000) and we spent another £90,000 (approximately U.S. $160,000) fixing it up. At the time, we were a church of about 50 young people—50 poor young people. We had neither the money nor the prospect of getting the money (legally), but we believed that God said He would look after us and that He would provide the money. So far, He has been doing just that. It has been an exciting 13 years, and at times we have wondered, *How are You going to do it now, Lord?* but we have seen again and again that God is powerful and trustworthy.

Yet what happens when you put your faith in the Lord and it doesn't work out? Let's be honest, it happens, and we are left asking "Why?" When Joseph dreamed of his brothers bowing down before him (see Gen. 37:5-11), was the dream not from God? In the end, the dream turned out to be correct, but Joseph had messed up the timing. We once promoted a tour and lost £14,000 (approximately U.S. $25,000). We were upset. Had we heard God wrong? Was it wrong to do the tour in the first place?

The truth is that God will have His will; God will do what He wants anyway. He cared more for me than He did for the tour not losing money. He was more interested in what He did in Joseph than what He did through Joseph. He put him through all that suffering, and Joseph came out of it not bitter, but better. When he met his brothers, he said, "Don't worry. You didn't do this to me. God sent me ahead of you, that through me you might be saved. What you did you meant for harm, but God meant it for good" (see Gen. 50:20).

Many years before that, when Joseph was in the middle of his nightmare, he chose to trust God. When Pharaoh said, "I hear you're good on dreams," common sense would have told Joseph to leave well alone and say, "No, Pharaoh, I used to be into dreams, but it hasn't done me any good, so I've given up on that one." Instead he said, "No, God gives the interpretation to dreams. I will ask God" (see Gen. 41:15-16). He continued to trust in what God had given him. The only way you get to succeed is by risking failure in the Christian faith. Many of us don't succeed because we are not willing to risk failure, and so we decide to settle for mediocrity. Faith is continuing to trust God in adversity, still believing Him when things go wrong. Without faith you just get bitter. Without faith you just go nowhere. Faith is what makes Christianity work.

Notes

1. "Blondin," *Encyclopædia Britannica*, Encyclopædia Britannica Premium Service. http://www.britannica.com/eb/article?tocId=9015693&query=wheelbarrow&ct= (accessed July 26, 2005).

2. Phil Campbell, "Believe it . . . or not?" Michelton Presbyterian Church Bible Teaching Resources. http://www.mpc.org.au/resources/resources/19990822.html (accessed July 26, 2005).

Chapter 6

CHOCOLATE AND OTHER EVILS
(A chapter about temptation)

Like the European Union, red states and blue states, the Los Angeles Lakers and the Manchester United soccer team, warfare is one of those topics on which opinion is well and truly divided. Many follow the path marked *Ignore It*, while others plumb for the one called *Adore It*. There have been many a time when I sweated away my teenage years picturing myself as a heavenly action hero getting stuck in a little one-on-one with some present problem. At other times I would walk along the Christian path, blissfully unaware that I was in the middle of the most violent of storms. A big fan of C. S. Lewis, I am living proof of Lewis's theory that the devil has two plans of attack: to get us to become obsessed with him or to cause us to be in a state of complete unbelief. So how do we live life without the obsessions or the ignorance? And if we do manage to work it out, what's the benefit to us anyway?

CHAPTER 6

Nehemiah and the Wall

The book of Nehemiah, although one of the lesser well-known Old Testament books, has the advantage of making this chapter seem very spiritual. (Now might be a good time for you to pick up your Bible and turn to the book of Nehemiah, just to see that I'm not lying.) Nehemiah tells his story, and throughout it we can see three classic ways in which Satan attacks the people of God. In fact, so classic are the attacks on Nehemiah that even today we seem to experience the same ones in the same order. Spooky. Throughout Nehemiah's story, we can see that for much of the time, warfare is about resisting temptation and focusing on God and not about trying to dismantle the enemy's kingdom ourselves.

Nehemiah was cupbearer to the king of Babylon at the time of the Jewish exile and lived in the citadel of Susa (the winter palace). One day Hanani, one of Nehemiah's brothers, arrives from Jerusalem and tells him all about life in Jerusalem. The situation is bad: Without decent walls, the city has fallen to ruins. And even though Ezra has been rebuilding it, every time progress is made, their enemies destroy the city. Time and time again Jerusalem has been plundered, leaving it a pale reflection of the grand city it once was. Nehemiah's response to Hanani's news is quick and simple: "When I heard these things, I sat down and wept. For some days I mourned and fasted and prayed before the God of heaven" (Neh. 1:4).

As we said in chapter 3, any work of God starts with weeping. It doesn't start with forming a committee, devising an action plan or chanting "Go for it!" 20 times an hour. This may sound a little foolish, but as Western Christians, we're keen on using our *Practical-DIY-Get-Up-and-Go-Let-Me-Sort-It-Out-God* skills and not so keen when it comes to sitting down and letting God take the lead. Practical problems don't always need our practical solutions.

Before being sent out to get his hands dirty, Nehemiah had his heart well and truly broken by God. Too often we try to go out and *do something* because we've been inspired by a talk, a sermon or a book, but the trouble is that we're going out without having been broken; we're leaving without full preparation for the journey. Many times we turn back half way, disillusioned, disenchanted or just plain distracted. Now I know that all sounds very neat and tidy with its three *D*s and all that, but letting God take the lead has to be the best way of making sure that you're doing the right thing.

Having wept, mourned and fasted for some days, Nehemiah then prays. What he says to God is an unusual yet fantastic prayer: He begins by praising Him and follows with a confession of the sins of his people. He confesses that he too has been a part of the wickedness and disobedience. For all we can tell, Nehemiah was a very righteous man who could easily have distanced himself from those who had done the real sinning. Instead he identifies with the people and avoids being patronizing. In a way, his words are an early illustration of the saying that the preaching of the gospel is simply one beggar telling another where to find food; we are all equal in our falling short of God's standards.

A while later, Nehemiah packs up and heads off to Jerusalem with the blessing of his king. (The trip would have taken three and a half months by camel, which means that he would have been forced to cut his ties with Susa.) Arriving in Jerusalem, Nehemiah checks out the city for a while and eventually lets the people in on his plan. He gets them fired up with the vision and they all begin work on rebuilding the wall. Once they start, they come under attack from their enemies—attacks of the type that we experience today.

First, we are introduced to Sanballat the Horonite and his pal Tobiah the Ammonite, who happens to be one of those sort of people who, at school, would have been mouthing off next to the school bully, too small to fight his own battles. In Nehemiah 4:3, Tobiah gets involved in an early round of ridicule, giving the builders a load of mouth about their wall not being strong enough for a fox to climb up on it. Similar to Tobiah, the enemy often attacks us with ridicule over the things about which we are most insecure. These subtle attacks get us where it hurts. Instead of the enemy making up something that is plainly untrue, he causes us to think, *Of course I couldn't do anything great for God. After all, I don't pray nearly enough and my Bible is covered in dust.* Having had thousands of years in which to work on this technique, the enemy seems to be doing pretty well at lying. Jesus said that Satan is a liar and the father of lies. That means he's a very good liar. His best lies are half-truths. I have never suffered from the sudden panic that God could never use me because I am anorexic: Look at me and you don't see anorexic. What I do go for though are thoughts about being disorganized, forgetful and a complete nightmare to work with. By feeding us a line that is partly true, the devil has a much better chance of making us swallow the whole lie.

Look at Nehemiah. He was a cupbearer, so he probably hadn't won many awards for wall construction. The joke about the fox probably was a bit too close for comfort and could easily have got him down. Instead, Nehemiah's reaction was spot on: Choosing not to argue about the merits of his particular building technique, he turned to God in prayer.

The second attack is the not-so-subtle full frontal assault that we read about in Nehemiah 4:7-11. The enemies band together and decide that the rebuilding is something that should be stopped immediately. They go so far as to threaten to murder the workers. At times we may encounter opposition: Perhaps someone may react to us with an unexpected and unreasonable level of anger. It may come from outside the Church or from within; it may be the result of hanging out with people from school or starting a new group in our church. Satan may even send illness to get us really freaked, and if he has it his way, we will give up, thinking that the blessing isn't flowing and we are not doing what God wants. This is a rubbish excuse. Just take a look at the Bible and it's easy to see that the signs of persecution (shipwrecks, imprisonment and torture) were for Paul the signs that he was in exactly the right place. God does want the best for us, but the best is not always the easiest—the best is being in the center of our Father's will.

What Nehemiah and his countrymen did was another great response to an attack. They prayed and posted a guard (see Neh. 4:9). They didn't just do the spiritual thing, nor did they lean exclusively on the practical; they found a balance.

As D. L. Moody once said, "When faced with a certain situation we should pray as if the entire outcome depended on God, and work as if it depended on us."

With such a good response to the second attack, though, you know that the third attack is not far off. In Nehemiah 6 the work is all done, apart from a little door hanging. It isn't hard to imagine that this collective of abused, oppressed and under-resourced builders would be feeling a little tired at this point and wide open to temptation. The enemies spread a few rumors and then offer a meeting and a chance to compromise on Nehemiah's earlier position. Nehemiah, refusing to give in, sees their attack for what it is and sends them away, praying for more strength to finish the job. Compromise for Nehemiah would have meant throwing away the potential of a mighty work of God. Accepting second best might leave us with an easier ride in the short term, but ultimately it is a waste of a life.

Unlike Nehemiah, you could say that the televangelists that fell so publicly in the early 1990s compromised with sin. The actual point of compromise may have been the sin that brought them down, or it may have happened long before that when they did away with the need for accountability.

My Dark Sin

I have an addiction. Since my early teens—when I was first introduced to it at school—I have been involved in a violent battle with cake. I have suffered attacks from all manner of confectionery and pastries; yet the one that grips my soul the tightest is the legendary *Triple Chocolate Surprise*. I make no apologies for what I am about to describe, though I hope that it may comfort a few.

One evening I returned to my flat having been away at an event. I was feeling tired and low, once again going through the turbulence of returning to normality, having been looked after so well the previous few days. After unpacking, I sat down and looked about me. I surveyed my home, feeling surprised that, as a reflection of my character, my flat seemed to focus more heavily on the chaotic and disorganized bits of me rather than on the highly intellectual and stylish bits that I knew were there in abundance. Midway through a thought about how much more dust it would take before I could use my coffee table as a mattress, my eyes landed on the fridge. My heart began to beat faster as I remembered what lay inside: a cake so rich and full of chocolate that I had found it necessary to make up an excuse to the shop assistant when I bought it about it being purely for medical research. I had not yet touched the cake, and it had been settling down in the fridge for a couple of days. It was such a beautiful piece of craftsmanship that I decided it would be good to just open the fridge door and gaze upon it, to take in the full glory. I decided I would only look.

What followed may be hard to believe, but I say nothing but the truth. It spoke to me. I remember the words as if they were uttered yesterday: "Hello, Mike," said the cake. Somewhat taken aback, I returned the greeting and we exchanged pleasantries. I invited the cake to join me on the kitchen table for a little meeting before bedtime. Slowly, I took it out of the fridge and sat down opposite it. Delicate beads of moisture formed on the side as it reacted to the heat of the room.

There followed one of those late night conversations you have with chocolate cake. After a while I said, "Listen, Cakie," (for we were becoming more relaxed in each other's company). "I have been wondering, are you defrosted?"

Cakie thought about this for a moment and then said, "I think so. The only way we will know is if you taste a little of my frosting and see."

I agreed, telling myself that tasting a little of Cakie's frosting is not really the same as eating Cakie. *Technically, it is not going all the way.* Tragically, however, one thing led to another and by the end of the evening, Cakie and I were one flesh.

I wish I could tell you that every mouthful tasted horrible, but it was exquisite. That's the trouble with sin. It always feels so enjoyable at the time. I reasoned that Cakie and I loved each other. *How could something that feels so right be so wrong? We were meant for each other.* It all felt good, in fact, until I had swallowed the last mouthful. Then I felt ill. The full horror hit me. "What have I done? I have eaten Cakie!" I was full of remorse, but it was too late. That is the second problem with sin: It may feel nice at the time, but the regret always comes later.

As I lay in my bed, watching the room brighten with the sun, I reflected on the cause of my fall from grace. *Where did I go wrong? Was it when I cut the first slice? Was it when I swapped the teaspoon for the desert spoon, thus enabling me to get more in my mouth each time? Was it when I gave up on cutlery altogether and used my hands to shove the cake in?* Then the truth came to me. The cause of my physical agony was the opening of the fridge door. Once I had the cake in view, there was no stopping me, and my problems had begun. Learn from my mistake. Don't open the fridge door. Once you do it, it is too late. If you are particularly susceptible to temptation, don't even go in the kitchen alone; take someone with you.

I think you may have guessed what I'm talking about here. I am referring to more than double chocolate cake—what about strawberry cheesecake, lemon meringue pie and apple pie and ice cream? Really, I am talking about sex before marriage. So be warned: Whatever your poison is, don't open the fridge door.

Elijah Meets God

Elijah was another person who came under a few attacks. Having sorted out the 450 prophets of Baal on the top of Mount Carmel, securing his title as *Undisputed Holy Man of the Year,* we find Elijah running away from a woman named Jezebel (see 1 Kings 18:16–19:4). He sat under a broom tree in the middle of the desert, wanting to die, and was in what can only be described as a big hole. How could that happen to one so tough? The similarities between Elijah and myself may not be immediately obvious, but I know how he feels. I know what it's like to wake up and feel like the richest man in the world. And who could be happier? I have great friends. I get paid to do a job I love, and I get to stand on platforms looking important. But sometimes I think I have absolutely nothing. I'll sit in my flat and run through my list: I'm a pastor. I'm over 40 and will soon reach my sell-by date—or maybe I already have and no one has told me. I'm single and may never marry. Who do I know who would be utterly devastated if I died? There may never be little Pilavachis running around the place. What am I going to do with the rest of my life?

Most of us know what this feels like. Elijah went through something that many of us experience when we return from the Soul Survivor festivals or some other great meeting or conference. Suddenly, the adrenaline stops flowing and the panic sets in. Elijah had experienced a *De Luxe Move of God* and was left feeling like a slug. God's response was not one that you would expect: He told Elijah to sleep and sent an angel with bread and water to tend to him, proving that God's spirituality is a lot more practical than ours (see 1 Kings 19:5-6). Not feeling like a spiritual giant when we are tired is not a sin; it's a simple reality.

God then took Elijah to a cleft in the mountain and gave him a display of raw power: an earthquake, a hurricane and a fire (see 1 Kings 19:11-13). However, God didn't choose to speak through them; instead, He used a gentle whisper. When Elijah heard the whisper, he put on his cloak and went back the way he came. The significance of this passage is huge. Through the experience, God taught Elijah that life isn't about the earthquakes, the experiences at Soul Survivor, the winds of this conference or the fire of that meeting; life is about finding Him in the ordinary and the mundane. When we have no big spiritual events acting as our support, it's vital that we can still hear His voice. Instead of having a relationship with His children through a collection of spiritual highs, God wants to be our life source.

Be Sensible

There are times when I go home after a meeting or service and I feel dreadful. Sleep is an impossibility and listening to the BBC World Service is my only entertainment. I may pace around the house for a while or try to read a book, but generally I'm too caught up in feeling bad about myself to concentrate on anything other than my sad life. I need to learn to find God in that place and pour out my heart to Him. I can also learn to anticipate when I am going to feel low and vulnerable to attack. A policeman friend of mine once gave me the best advice that he knew: In a conflict, run. There's nothing wrong with avoiding those situations in which we know that the enemy is going to have a good chance at knocking us off balance.

Turn Off the Darkness

For some, perhaps this idea of focusing on God and avoiding the attacks may not seem much like warfare. Where is the battle against darkness? Where are the encounters with the demons? Paul experienced his fair share of opposition; you could say he was a seasoned warrior. For all his experience, he chose to find the balance between ignorance and obsession. When he wrote to the church at Ephesus, he mentioned that ours is not a fight against flesh and blood but against the "principalities, against powers, against the rulers of the darkness of this age" (Eph. 6:12, *NKJV*). He lists the weapons with which to fight, yet when he arrived in Ephesus, a city that was a center of demonic activity (even the economy was based on demonology—see Acts 19:23-27), he didn't hide himself in a room and charge up on a little one-on-one with the local principalities or powers. Instead, he spread the Kingdom by preaching the gospel and healing the sick. Demons were cast out, but Paul concentrated on building the Church rather than dismantling the enemy (see Acts 19:8-12).

Watford, England, has a history of disunity between churches, and when we started Soul Survivor Watford we anticipated a fair amount of hostility. From one couple, though, we got the exact opposite: Instead of warning people off about us, Gordon and Rachel Hickson (the pastors of Watford Community Church) told some of their people to come and visit us. "I may well lose them to you," Gordon told me, "but I don't care." A little confused, we asked him to explain. He told us that when they had arrived in Watford, they had seen all the opposition between the churches. They then decided that they were going to live in the opposite spirit that they were going to be generous and try to bless all the other churches. Since then, the churches have come together, united against the enemy. That's warfare.

Imagine going to live in Soho, one of the truly seedy areas of London. Instead of moving into a flat and combating the powers of sexual perversion and immorality by shadowboxing the demons from your front room, wouldn't it be better to live in the opposite spirit? Where people are greedy, you could be generous; where there is immorality, you could be pure; and where there is an absence of hope, you could instill self-worth and pride. That too would be warfare.

We need to read the Bible—the truth—in order to resist the enemy's lies. In Luke 4:1-13, we read about the temptation of Jesus in the desert. He was tempted by the devil, and He was tempted when He was at His weakest. I struggle if I have fasted between breakfast and lunch. Jesus had been at it for 40 days. He was hungry. He was tired. After 40 days in the desert, He would have been in desperate need of comfort.

The devil chose his moment. The devil always chooses his moments. He tempted Jesus at His absolute weakest and said, "If you are the Son of God, tell this stone to become bread" (v. 3) If I had been in Jesus' place, I would have thought, *I have been spiritual for 40 whole days; one loaf of bread won't do me any harm*. But Jesus answered, "It is written: 'Man does not live on bread alone'" (v. 4). There came two other temptations, each to which Jesus answered, "It is written . . . " (see vv. 8,12). One of the biggest helps in resisting temptation is to know the Word, to live the Word and to let the Word live in you. It would have been very difficult for Jesus to say "It is written" if He hadn't known what had been written.

In John's Gospel, Jesus told the disciples that when they were in need, the Holy Spirit would remind them of every-thing He had told them (see John 14:26). That promise is for us as well. But the Holy Spirit cannot remind us if we do not know it in the first place. In Ephesians 6:17, we are told that the sword of the spirit is the Word of God. We need to be equipped with the sword of the spirit, knowing that the Word gives us a reference point outside of our feelings when the temptations are strong.

Perhaps God could have done things a little differently 2,000 years ago. Perhaps He could have had a heavenly battle against the darkness, but instead He chose to send down some purity, send down some light. In His life, Jesus offers a perfect model of living in a countercultural way; while at times He confronted the enemy head-on, for the most part He spread love, forgiveness and relationship with God.

Chapter 7

EVERYBODY LOVES A LOVER
(A chapter about being family)

If the first and greatest commandment is that we love the Lord our God with all our heart, soul, mind and strength, then the second greatest is not far off: that we love our neighbor as ourselves. Jesus knew that we would probably need things explained a little, so He carried on, making it into a whole new commandment: "My command is this: Love each other as I have loved you. Greater love has no one than this, that he lay down his life for his friends. You are my friends if you do what I command" (John 15:12-14). The command suddenly becomes even harder to fulfill as Jesus throws in the bit about being as good at loving as He is. It makes me wonder why Jesus felt the need to give a new commandment to the disciples just before He died. Perhaps the answer is that He knew the Church would not survive if the new Christians (His disciples) did not love one another with something approaching the same depth and commitment that He had shown them.

It took me quite a while to realize that the parts in the Bible that are labeled as commands are not just the optional extras that you can take or leave as the mood suits. I spent many years forgiving people about as often as I washed out my lunch box. Due to a particularly bad bout of internal fungus, I realized one day that Jesus gave commands because He meant His people to do what He said. If we know what is good for us, we will try to be His disciples—taking the commands that He gave to the first 12 as our own.

Yet what does it mean to love one another as Jesus loves us? The culture from which Jesus came is far removed from ours, so how can we find the connection between His actions and our possibilities? In order to understand this, we need to return to Jesus' initial comments about loving one another. He explains Himself more fully by saying, "Greater love has no one than this, that he lay down his life for his friends." On one level, Jesus was talking about what He was about to do: go to the cross on behalf of His friends and loved ones. But going to the cross wasn't just an isolated act of kindness. Jesus took up His cross long before He was captured. He continually laid down His life by preferring the disciples. While it may not result in crucifixion, we are called to lay down our lives for each other, putting others first, with our own needs and preferences taking second place. Even though Jesus was the Son of God, He treated His disciples not only as equals but even as superiors. He calls us to be servants of one another as He was a servant to us.

A Guide to Loving Each Other Like Jesus Loved Us (In Four Parts)

Part 1—To Be Vulnerable

The first way that Jesus loved the disciples was by being vulnerable before them. Vulnerability is a hard concept for Western people to accept. Many of us (particularly men from an English culture) have been brought up to think that showing emotion is as embarrassing as a fart on a crowded train. We would rather spend our lives as prisoners to this way of living than share with others our grief, pain and fear. We seem to be taking our cue from the two Jameses: James Bond and Captain James T. Kirk. Yet Jesus did not live like that; His was not a model of Lone Ranger Christianity. We should not look to the examples of emotional constipation. Jesus showed us another way: gathering His people around Him and sacrificing every part of Himself for them.

Jesus was not only vulnerable but was also willing to show His vulnerability through His actions. He not only felt things deeply, but He also was willing for people to see what He felt. He wept over Jerusalem and He wept over His friend Lazarus (see Luke 19:41; John 11:35). It amazes me not so much that Jesus wept over the city and over a man, but that He allowed people to see Him weep. Many of us do our weeping in private, cleaning up and putting on a smile when we're in public. Jesus showed His vulnerability in the garden of Gethsemane when He told Peter, James and John, "My soul is overwhelmed with sorrow to the point of death" (Matt. 26:38). There was vulnerability on the cross when He allowed people to strip Him naked, laugh at Him and taunt Him (see Matt 27:27-31).

Many of us are afraid of being vulnerable because of one simple equation: vulnerability equals pain. There is no way around the fact that if we make ourselves vulnerable, we will be hurt. But what makes us so special that we should have an easier deal than Jesus? He called us to live lives of vulnerability with each other, and that means risking pain and hurt as He did. As followers of Christ, we are meant to engage with one another as He did, because He did.

There are three pictures of the Church that I have heard and thought about. Colin Urquhart came up with the first one years ago. He wrote that churchgoers are like snooker balls that come out of their pockets on Sunday, bounce off each other, and then say "clickerty-click, Amen" before returning down the holes. Next Sunday, there they are, bouncing and clicking, giving it a bit of "Amen" and then returning to pocket land. Then one Sunday, the church gets excited and interested in the things of the Spirit. From that point on, the churchgoers come out of their pockets and say "clickerty-click, Amen, praise the Lord, Hallelujah" and then go back down the holes. They are still hard on the outside, despite being filled with the Spirit on the inside. Sadly, some churches are like that, full of fired-up people who refuse to be vulnerable with each other.[1]

An evangelist from Argentina named Juan Carlos Ortis told me about his idea of another picture of the Church, but this time it was of how it should be. He called it "Mashed Potato Love." God takes a whole load of spuds, hard and individual, and peels them, boils them, and then mashes them together. That is how God wants His people to be: not individual hard potatoes, separate from one another, but one glorious mound of creamy mash. In many ways it's a wonderful picture, but it does give the idea that we lose our individuality by being part of the Body.

A picture I prefer is one that a friend of mine told me about some years ago. He saw the Church as a honeycomb made up of hundreds of six-sided cells, with each cell being in direct contact with six others. If one cell in the honeycomb were damaged, all the others around would be affected. My friend felt that this was how the Church should be: maintaining individuality yet encouraging a strong bond between each of the members. So, as in a honeycomb, if one cell laughs, the others should feel the vibrations. If one cell cries, all the others should get wet. This is what Paul understood when he wrote to the Romans and advised them to "rejoice with those who rejoice; mourn with those who mourn" (Rom. 12:15). The unity between us as Christians is supposed to be that strong.

Part 2—To Forgive
The second way that Jesus loved His disciples was by forgiving them. Jesus told us to love one another as He loved us, so we need to forgive as Jesus forgave. The chances are that this will become a regular occurrence; for as we make ourselves vulnerable to others, we come across the old "vulnerability equals pain" rule again, as people let us down. Having been hurt, the only healthy reaction that we can put into place is to forgive.

I have found forgiveness to be the hardest part of being a Christian. Inasmuch as the English are born with the legacy of the stiff upper lip, we Greeks come into the world with the words "never forgive" imprinted on our hearts. I managed to work at it a little bit and soon found that when a stranger hurt me, it was not too difficult to grant them my cleansing forgiveness. However, if a friend does something to hurt me, it is a very different story. Normally my first reaction is simple but effective: I decide not to forgive. I follow this up with a swift dose of ignorance, trying as hard as I can to put the situation out of mind.

The trouble starts when I end up in a worship meeting. I may be in the middle of singing a tender song to Jesus when all of a sudden I start thinking about that Judas, the one that hurt me. Again I try to wipe him from my memory, but it seems as though God is saying, "You can't worship me unless you forgive this person." A struggle usually follows and eventually I end up giving in (the odds are slightly stacked against me, after all). Having forgiven him, I feel better—the awkward feeling in the pit of my stomach being replaced with a little peace and lovely, fluffy, bouncy thoughts.

This state usually lasts for about one minute. I soon remember why I had to forgive him in the first place and I'm back at square one, although this time feeling even angrier that I had been fooled into forgiving him. "Forgive that person again," says the Lord. So I do and things are lovely, fluffy and bouncy again.

Until the next time I see him. If it happens to be out somewhere and everyone is laughing except him, crying in a corner on his own, then I find it surprisingly easy to maintain my high standard of forgiveness. But if he happens to be the center of attention, that twisted feeling starts up in my stomach again and I can see no reason why I should let him off the hook. *After all*, I reason to myself, *if I did forgive him, he would obviously not learn his lesson. If it weren't for my sharp stings of correction, how would he ever grow?* At times I feel like God's ambassador, put on Earth to do the dirty work of showing people the consequences of their sin. God's reply is swift: "Quiet—that's My job. Because I forgave you, you must forgive them."

Perhaps my scenario is not so ridiculous, for one of the disciples once asked Jesus how many times we should forgive. The disciple suggests the figure seven. I may be missing the point here, but what on Earth made him think of seven? Apart from Matthew (the tax collector) and Judas, the disciples were not very good at math, and a man of that caliber would probably have been foxed by Jesus' answer: "I do not say to you, up to seven times, but up to seventy times seven" (Matt. 18:22, *NKJV*)—which basically means that we are to forgive all the time. We are supposed to forgive each person until the hurt goes away (not, as I used to think, only 490 different people). If we are honest, that can be a long time. But in sending His Son to the cross, God gave us a clear answer to a simple question: How much do we deserve forgiveness?

We need to practice forgiveness, to learn how to continually forgive people even though they might be (a) unrepentant, (b) unaware or (c) better looking. Sadly, the consequence of not forgiving is that we become bitter and twisted as their fault becomes our problem. They may not be aware, or even care, that you want to kill them. The only person who gets screwed up is you, and the relationship that gets most screwed up is the relationship between you and God.

Part 3—To Serve

Jesus also showed His love for the disciples by choosing to serve them. There was one time when Jesus and the disciples arrived at a place after having been out in the desert (see John 13). It seems that the servants had the day off, so there was nobody around of low enough rank to get down and wash peoples' feet. Jesus took a towel and some water and He got down on His knees and got on with the job. "Now that I, your Lord and Teacher, have washed your feet, you should also wash one another's feet," He said (v. 14).

Back when I was a youth pastor, this seemed like a great illustration of servanthood. So one day, I decided to re-create the moment with my youth group. We were away at the time, and the night before I told them what we were going to do the next day so that nobody would be embarrassed whipping off their socks and suffocating everyone else in the vicinity. We had done a little homework and turned up prepared; we had plenty of hot water, clean towels, individual bowls and a lifetime's supply of both Passion Fruit and Limestone Foot Creams. That morning, we split into pairs to wash each other's feet. We all were moved by the experience of having another person serving us in such a way and then by returning the favor. We finished with a wise thought that I had prepared: "Now that is exactly what Jesus did 2,000 years ago."

A few days later, I thought about my closing speech and realized that what we had done was nothing like what Jesus had done 2,000 years ago. Jesus didn't actually say to the disciples, "I'm on wash duty tomorrow, so make sure you all have a good scrub beforehand." Nor did he say that he was about to produce a superb sermon illustration and it would be very much appreciated if they could all pay attention and not do anything silly to spoil it. There was a reason why the disciples sat around saying, "I'm not doing the washing." Having been out in the desert, their feet were hardly a vision of loveliness—sweat, mud, blood and worse would have been more like it. Washing people's feet was usually the job of the lowest servant, the one who amounted to nothing; yet this time Jesus put Himself out.

There are all sorts of ways in which we can serve others. One of my favorite techniques is the *Humble Yet Highly Visual*. I believe that I could go head to head with the most servant-hearted of people as long as there was a good crowd to cheer me on. But when I play to a heavenly audience of One, I find things a little harder work.

When I first joined Saint Andrews Chorleywood, I traveled there by train from my home in Harrow. This soon became a pain. One day, I was whining to my friend Chris about it. He suggested that we pray about it, and we asked God to find me somewhere to stay, if only for a short while. A few days later, I had a call from two ladies in the church asking me to housesit for them while they went on a six-week trip to New Zealand. I agreed and was totally amazed. I was soon on the phone to Chris telling him about this fantastic answer to prayer. He was really pleased too and said it was great the way the Lord answers prayer.

I had a great time while the two ladies were away. I had just about managed to replace all the food by the time they returned home, and we sat around and chatted before I left. "There was one thing that was puzzling me," I said. "Why did you ask me to housesit?"

"Didn't you know?" they replied. "Chris suggested your name. He said you would make a great housesitter."

That bowled me over. There was no way that Chris would have let me know, and I only found out by accident. If it had been me, I would surely have turned on the charm with the old "Oh please, it was nothing. You would have done the same for me. It was a bit difficult getting you a place to stay mind you, but I persuaded them and put my name on the line for you." But there was nothing in it for Chris, just the simple act of being a servant. God works in a similar way: loving us because of His love, not because of the buzz He gets.

Part 4—To Be Honest

Jesus also loved His disciples by being honest with them. The verse in Ephesians that mentions speaking the truth in love (see Eph. 4:15) is often misused to justify behavior that isn't Christlike. At a church I used to attend, there was one man who seemed to make a habit of catching my eye and heading straight for me, releasing into the air the magic words "Now I say this in love, brother." It was as if he thought those very words would turn whatever criticism that followed into pearls of great wisdom. Far from having me fall to my knees in humbled privilege to have been enlightened by this *great man of God*, the "I say this in love" warning had me on my knees faking a heart attack in the hope that he might leave well enough alone and prey on someone else.

Thankfully, the true meaning of the verse is a little different. To speak the truth in love means first of all to speak positive and affirming truth. I'm not talking about saying schmaltzy, honey-covered things like "I think you're like a lovely little lamb and your bleating is like an angel's harp." The truth is nothing if it is not honest. We find this hard to do; it seems to contradict our nature of being strong and independent, as if by acknowledging someone else's strength we admit our weakness.

On another occasion years ago, I talked with my youth group about encouraging one another with things that were honest and true. To illustrate it, each of them took a piece of paper and wrote their names at the top. They then passed the sheets around and wrote on each other's pages one thing that would be an encouragement to that person.

This was the most buzzing thing we had ever done in the youth group. *Bless them*, I thought, *these little ones obviously needed affirming*. I thanked God that I was mature enough not to need to take part. Then one of them called my bluff and asked me if I was joining in. For the sake of setting an example, I joined in, fully intending just to glance at my sheet some time over the next few months. When everyone had finished writing, they took their sheets and read through the 22 reasons why the others liked them.

The loudest lad in the group went into a corner and stayed there for 20 minutes, reading and rereading what was written on the paper. It was as if he was drinking it in. At the end, he came up to me and asked if I could help him work out which person had written which comment. Even six months later they still had those pieces of paper, pinned on their walls or stuck in their Bibles.

Bless them, I thought as they left, *they obviously needed that.* Then I ran upstairs and tore open my piece of paper, reading it over and over, trying to work out which comment belonged to which person. None of us is too old, too mature or too secure to pass up on a bit of affirmation. We are meant to affirm others because it reflects the character of Jesus.

There is, however, another side to speaking the truth in love, because sometimes we all need a little guidance as we fumble our way along the path. There isn't much worse than hearing the hard truth about ourselves from an enemy, especially if he or she is a good enemy, in which case he or she is bound to make sure that what is said really hurts. Infinitely preferable is hearing those hard truths from a friend—as the old saying goes, "Faithful are the wounds of a friend." Delivering the truth in this way does not mean verbally assaulting someone once the all-purpose "I say this in love" line has been added. Our words should come out of a caring and compassionate heart, the test of which is to ask yourself, "Do I enjoy pointing this 'problem' out to my friend?" If the answer is yes, then you should keep quiet and go back to torturing field mice. If it hurts you to say it, then you care more about the person than you care about getting it off your chest. We receive correction much better from those who we know love us.

A Helpful Saying

It seems funny, but the things that stick with you from a talk are often the most annoying. I picked this up years ago and have been winding people up with it ever since. Still, it makes a valid point, and if we followed it religiously we would probably never utter another word. Here goes:

Before you speak, *think*—is it

True,
Helpful,
Inspiring,
Necessary and
Kind?

If your words are not all of those things, shut your mouth.

Done the right way, it can be a liberating experience to hear caring words of guidance from a friend. It can bless us and strengthen our relationship with each other. I know my friends will tell me when something hasn't gone right; so when they affirm me and tell me that something was good, I am even more inclined to believe what they say. I know that they are not just being nice for the sake of it, because I know they would tell me if I had given a bad talk or if I was out of order. These relationships help me grow, which is what friendship and, ultimately, the Church should always be aiming for.

Lean On Me

These days, friendship is hard to find. Those real, true, long-lasting friendships seem to be fading into the past like bad fashion. The modern relationship has taken on the spirit of the age: consumerism. We treat friendships little better than a new jacket; at the slightest sign of a flaw or a defect, we take it back and demand a more perfect product. Once it has worn thin with age, we simply buy a replacement. The tragedy is that some people seem to have closer friendships with people from the other side of the world who they meet in Internet chat rooms and news groups than they do with the people living in the same time zone. As the Church, we need to work on our friendships; we need to work on expressing the love of God with one another, and when we do, our actions will speak loudly to others.

Jazz and the Great Commandment

It can seem confusing why Jesus decided to add this *loving one another* commandment just before He died. Would it not have been more sensible to introduce it a little earlier on in the campaign and give it a little more airtime? Perhaps it has the maximum power possible in the present form; Jesus tells His disciples to love as He has loved and follows up with the most dramatic display of love the world has ever seen. Like any parent, it gives God great pleasure when His children get along—and so, true friendship becomes part of our worship. John says in his first letter that if we say we love God but hate our brother, we are liars and the truth is not in us (see 1 John 1:5-7).

Those are strong words, but loving God must spill over into loving others, both those who are within the Church and those who aren't.

Another reason Jesus gave the new commandment was that it was the issue on which He wanted the world to judge us: "By this all men will know that you are my disciples, if you love one another" (John 13:35). There have been many examples of Christians hating each other, and each one has brought forth an army of critics. By Jesus' own words, their claims are justified. People look at our lives, not just our words. When a loving, caring society is what is being shown, it might not provoke quite as much noise, but something about it draws people in, intrigued and wanting to know more.

Many a night as a teenager, I whiled away in my room, nodding and tapping away to the jazz sounds of Shorty Rogers and his Orchestra featuring The Giants as they swung their way through a fired-up rendition of that Allen-Adler classic "Everybody Loves a Lover." Old Shorty certainly knew a thing or two about jazz, and this song title touched on a truth that we can all relate to: We do love lovers. More important, though, God loves lovers; we are meant to be lovers of God and (in the best way possible) lovers of each other. That is a definition of family and is how healing comes to the Church. I know that I have received much healing through brothers and sisters who have stood by me through thick and thin. One of the joys I have at Soul Survivor is that the people I work with have been my friends for over 10 years. We've seen the worst of each other; we've had our arguments, and yet we are still together. That length of time gives us a security and an honesty that can heal and support in ways that once seemed impossible. God has spoken to me about His commitment to me through the commitment of others to me. In return, I want to love others in the way that Jesus loves me.

Note

1. Colin Urquhart, *Anything You Ask* (London: Hodder and Stoughton; 2001), n.p.

Chapter 8

I AM A FIVE-COW WOMAN
(A chapter about self-image)

THE STORY

I once heard a student being interviewed on the radio about what he did in his Gap year, which is the year students take off between high school and college or university in England, and he talked about how he actually spent his time traveling around the world soaking up the experiences that life offered him. When I was at school, people didn't even take a whole year off; they just spent three months in Scotland.

This traveler was telling the DJ about his first destination, which was Indonesia. If I hadn't been so petrified of flying, I would have grown increasingly jealous at his descriptions of remote islands with white sands and turquoise seas. The traveler wanted to get as involved in the culture as possible, so he traveled to the most remote island he could find.

On the boat trip to the island, he noticed a group of locals laughing hysterically. Through an interpreter, he asked them what was going on. On this particular island—and I make no comment about it—the people had a custom that a woman's hand in marriage was paid for in cows by the groom. There had been no inflation for centuries, and the going rate for an average woman's hand in marriage would set you back about two and a half moo moos. The most that had ever been paid was five cows for the most beautiful and perfect woman the island had ever seen. The least was half a cow, which was a cow with parts dropping off that was well past its sell-by date. The islanders were all laughing because there was one man who had actually paid five cows for a wife who, really, could only ever be considered a three cow-er. The islanders said he had been conned by her father, and they all found it particularly funny.

Once the student was on the island, he made up his mind to find the man with such poor bartering skills and let him know what people were saying. Eventually the two met, and our English friend tactfully and gently told the man that he was a fool with no concept of what a good woman was worth. "Ah yes," was the reply. "I paid for my wife what I wanted to pay for her, and I paid what I thought she was worth. To me she is worth every udder, and when she walks through the village, she walks with her head held high. She says to herself, *I am a five-cow woman*. And because she believes that she is worth five cows, she acts like she is worth five cows and she even looks like she is worth five cows."

Many of us struggle because we don't know how much we are worth—many of us think our worth doesn't even get near half a cow but hovers around the half pint of semi-skimmed-milk mark. Instead of letting Jesus value us, we try to estimate our value on our own. Some of us work it out by the amount of money we have, some by our looks, others by our jobs or friends. If we measure our worth by these values, we're in trouble. The good news of the gospel is that God has shown, through the death of His Son on the cross, exactly how much we are worth to Him.

The reason why the rates of suicide, anorexia, bulimia and depression have shot up is that we are a generation of people who do not know our worth. We ride an emotional seesaw: At one end we are the sons and daughters of the King of kings, and at the other we are the products of a broken and fallen world. Somewhere in the middle there is a balance, but all too often we are weighed down and broken.

The Conversation

With both Craig Borlase and me being male, we thought we should get a female perspective on this subject, so here is Emily, a friend from our church. Emily holds a Certificate in Counseling and works for Social Services.

Mike Pilavachi: I reckon one of the main problems we face today is that we don't think we're worth very much. What do you think?

Emily Barnet: I think that the creation story shows that from the moment we humans sinned, we became insecure. As Adam and

Eve stood naked and vulnerable, they felt the urge to cover up and hide. From that day on humanity has done the same thing, hiding our real selves and putting up defenses. I suppose that because we are no longer in a perfect relationship with God, we don't feel safe and we feel the need to protect ourselves. There are lots of things we hide behind, like being the funny one or the quiet one, or by becoming aggressive.

MP: It might be hard to believe, but I was the funny kid at school. I'd tell jokes and act like the fool just to get people to like me. It was the exact opposite of what I was really like; at school I would be Mr. Funny, but I'd get home and I'd cry.

EB: I've seen that where I work. Children whose behavior is really difficult will burst into tears and tell me all their problems as soon as they are alone. The worst behaved child in the group once said he wanted to kill himself. He was eight years old. I know that there's a bit of me that thinks nobody would like the real me, so I apologize a lot before someone gets the chance to criticize me.

MP: I know someone who so wants to be loved that he takes on everybody's pain and is always the rescuer. He will always put himself in a place where he is needed, and at first you think that he is an amazing person, so helpful and considerate. But the truth is that he couldn't cope if he wasn't needed. He does good things but out of bad feelings.

EB: I don't think that the need to be needed always helps the other person.

MP: Yeah, it makes that person dependent.

EB: The reason that someone is being helped isn't because the helper wants that person to get better; it's because the helper wants to feel better. If the person being helped ever does get sorted out, the helper won't be needed. I think that sometimes the helper will keep the other person a few steps away from sorting things out just so that the helper isn't left alone, without anyone's problems to solve.

MP: There's quite a bit of talk these days about disorders like anorexia, bulimia and cutting, especially among younger people. Even though it's dangerous to generalize, what's your take on these disorders?

EB: When I was training to be a counselor, we talked about each of those things as being a way of acting out very strong feelings. Say you were brought up in a family where there was a lot of violence and anger; you might decide that anger is bad and vow not to express it. That's your defense, but it won't work because to feel angry is human; we all feel anger, and we all need it. So what do you do when you feel angry? You suppress it, but the feelings have to come out somewhere, and that might be through drinking, depression, anorexia or whatever. Often, people who are anorexic will say that they feel out of control, and so, although their life is full of pain, they can make themselves feel better by controlling something manageable—their eating. Going without food may make them feel better superficially but ignores the real struggles within. The person who suffers from bulimia might feel worthless and empty inside but have no way of expressing it. Binging might be a comfort, but then comes the feeling of guilt, which also can't be expressed; so the only way of dealing with that feeling of guilt is to make yourself sick.

MP: That causes a cycle: You feel bad; then you feel better for a short while, but then you find yourself back where you started.

EB: In a way, I think that you can generalize about acting out. Even violence is a way of getting rid of anger but without expressing it verbally, without confronting it and dealing with it.

MP: Being sexually promiscuous can be part of it too. Some may just like sleeping around, but I remember one girl who came to an event that our church put on who was so sexually charged that she did nothing but flirt with the guys. The way she teased them baffled me, and I had no idea why she did it. She then started coming to our meetings, where she would cry. She told me that someone in her family had sexually abused her when she was younger. She needed to know that she had power over men because they had caused so much pain in her own life. She was absolutely petrified of getting too close, which made her even more confused: She would sleep around, but she couldn't get close emotionally. When she met Jesus she began to sort things out.

EB: How can meeting Jesus sort things out?

MP: Well, this girl is a good example. During the worship she would cry, even though she didn't have a clue why. I remember her saying that things hurt too much for her to cope. Alcohol was a way out, and she would get drunk to counterbalance the pain. She reminded me of the film *Educating Rita* from the 1980s, in which one character tries to commit suicide. Rita asks this character why she did it when she had everything. The character tells her that when the highs of her life faded, she was left with herself "and that's not enough." With this girl at church, the sex was a cover-up too. In the end, Jesus made her face up to the real issues and the pain. We asked her if she wanted to ask Jesus into her life and she said that she was scared, that she had promised herself years before that she would never trust another man again. In asking Him in, she had to break her vow. It hasn't been easy sailing, but her life has been better for it.

EB: As you said, she had made a promise, and we often tell ourselves things over and over again that are very unhelpful. This can be difficult when we look to Jesus for healing, because we are the aspirin generation: We want it all made better right here, right now. Often Jesus will break in and perform a miraculous healing on the spot, but we also have a responsibility to work on things ourselves. If something is so deep-rooted, if it has affected so much of our lives, it may take us a while to learn to live differently, to live better.

MP: We have seen people at the Soul Survivor summer camps who have come with such great emotional damage that you wonder how they could ever be healed. But Jesus seems to do it; He loves to heal—and just as with everything else covered in this book, we need to find the balance between taking responsibility for our own lives and allowing God time and space to work on us.

EB: We mustn't deny the place of the instant and the miraculous healing, but we also must not ignore the role of the Church in being a place where we can get long-term support and fellowship.

MP: I know that there have been specific times in my life when I have received emotional healing. The first John Wimber conference in 1981 had me down in the front as what felt like waves of love washed over me, and something fantastic would happen. There have been other times like that, but I also know that if I didn't have friends around me as I have for 10 years—people who have seen the worst of me but who have stayed with me—I would be walking with a much worse limp than the one I have now.

EB: It can be powerful when we treat people like they've never been treated before. That's what Jesus did; He called Zaccheus down from the tree and ate with him—nobody had ever done that to Zaccheus. By valuing and spending time with each of the disciples, I'm sure Jesus laid a vital foundation.

MP: Bearing in mind that everything that Jesus did was of value, what was more significant: feeding the 5,000 with 5 pieces of bread and 2 sardines, or living with 12 disciples for 3 years? Who were the heroes in the Acts of the apostles? We may never know what happened to the 5,000, but it's pretty clear how Jesus' friendship affected those whom He was closest to. Both are good—the miraculous and the consistent, but it is important that Jesus did both.

I love the story of the woman caught in adultery. Jesus didn't say to her, "I accept you as you are; your lifestyle's not that bad." He looked up from the ground, where He was writing in the dirt, and told anyone who thought they were without sin to throw the first stone. When they had all gone, He told her to go and sin no more. Someone once said to me that they felt more accepted in a pub than in a church. This is a tragedy, at least to the degree that the statement is true. Our job is not to condemn—it doesn't mean compromising on sin, but we are not here to do God's job.

There was the Samaritan woman at the well who Jesus treated with great dignity even though there were three things wrong with her: she was a Samaritan, she was a sinner (she had had five husbands and the one she was with was not her husband) and she was a woman (the boys in their Bar Mitzvahs then would pray this prayer: "Lord God, thank you that you have not made me a Gentile; Lord God, I thank you that you have not made me a slave; Lord God, I thank you—oh how I thank you— that you have not made me a woman.") In that cultural context, Jesus treated her with dignity and respect. There can be real healing in something as simple as that.

As well as anorexia and bulimia, I have many friends who have suffered from panic attacks. The attacks were caused by many things, ranging from fear of death to fear of trains, sex or work.

EB: I didn't know much about it until it happened to me. I'd had a very secure upbringing and couldn't point to any one time when I felt things were terrible. I went off to medical school full of confidence but really struggled once I got there. Partly things were difficult because I was away from the things that were secure in my life, but mostly it was because I began to realize what drove and motivated me, and that was other peoples' expectations. I was a "sorry" person, constantly apologizing, believing the way to get by was to get approval from people, and that meant doing whatever they expected. While there wasn't one person who was setting these standards, I think I was making myself reach for the sky.

The work at college was harder and more frequent than any I had experienced before and it didn't take long before I felt completely out of my depth. During my exams at the end of the first term I had panic attacks. I remember waking up in the middle of the night, petrified that I was going to fall out of the window. The attacks were so intense that I would often get a friend to sit with me until I calmed down. The attacks came more often, and at the start of summer I told my parents that I was going to leave college—something in me knew that the two things were related.

Over the summer I calmed down, so I went back to school in September. Immediately the panic attacks returned and I was gripped with this fear of letting people down and being a disappointment to everyone. I became afraid of all sorts of strange things, such as being on my own, going on trains or being around knives. Eventually, I phoned my pastor and he totally shocked me by telling me that I didn't have to be at college. I had been working under the belief that being at college was exactly what I did need to be doing—how else was I going to please people? That was a real turning point, and he sent me off to have a chat with one of the doctors in the church. I told the doctor all about my fears and was kind of prepared for him to pack me off to the psychiatric ward. Instead, he said that my head was like a pressure cooker—there were all these expectations on me but no way of letting the steam out. He told me that a panic attack does just that, releases the stress when it has gotten to be too much. Unless you deal with the cause of the anxiety, you are bound to have irrational fears. I thought that I was dealing with my fears by giving in to them, but really I was letting them take over and control my life.

That day was an amazing day—I felt an amazing sense of freedom at the end of it, but it then took months for me to start looking at the roots of what had caused the problems in the first place. I had missed the point about what I was worth. I thought that my work was the only way that I was going to get God's approval.

Sometimes we can read a chapter like this and think that it's fine for others to look inside themselves and understand what's going on, but as for us, we don't know how we feel; we don't even know if we feel anything at all. It's a common enough problem particularly among young men. They have been brought up with male role models who have the old stiff upper lip.

MP: I'm worried that it will only be the girls who read this chapter. We have somehow come to a point where men think they don't need to express themselves, and I think that's very dangerous. We need to encourage young men to believe that it is okay to look in on the feminine side and feel things deeply.

EB: Haven't we seen this at church, where the girls find it so much easier to build relationships than the boys . . .

MP: But when the guys do make strong and supportive friendships, it's fantastic.

EB: I wonder whether we know what it is to be a man these days? Back in the 1950s—however good or bad it was—the man had a clearly defined role as the breadwinner, with an established position in society. Today we have more and more women in the workplace—which is a fantastic thing—but more and more men are wondering what use they are. In no way am I suggesting that locking women up in the kitchen will bring the male suicide rate down, but I think we have a responsibility to be aware of the climate and be ready to understand how men feel these days.

MP: I don't think that men and women competing for a job is wrong, but I do think that some of the more intense girl power stuff is actually belittling to men. Men and women are different; that's where the attraction lies, but when the differences are ignored it gets tough.

The answer to all of this is first to discover what God thinks of us; to discover that our value is more than just a few pounds of flesh and bone; to discover that we are worth more than two and a half cows. I think God is saying to us, "If you want to know how much you're worth, look at the Cross. I went out and bought you, and I paid the price with the life of my Son." It can be hard to accept His valuation. When you've always believed that you're worth nothing, it's a heck of a job to believe that you're worth the life of Jesus. That's why we need to discover more of God through worship and through our friendships. As the second commandment is to love our neighbor as we love ourselves, we cannot truly love our neighbor unless we know our own worth.

EB: Sometimes the solution really is that practical. We need to find those verses that say how much we're worth; we need to find someone who can pray things through with us. It isn't always that easy though; some people are in a church where there doesn't seem to be anyone to turn to.

MP: Yes, that's hard, but building those relationships is so important. There might be someone from another church or school or college, but as long as he or she can be trusted, sometimes all it takes is having someone who is willing to listen and then pray with you. That person doesn't need to be a wonderful prophet or preacher; just find someone who will be there. I'm not saying that working through any of this stuff is easy, but it is so worth the effort. Ultimately, living a life for God is all about becoming more like Jesus, giving God the chance to restore us to the people He intended us to be.

Chapter 9

LEARNING TO CATCH
(A chapter about healing)

God wants more than anything to have His children turn back to Him. But it doesn't stop there; once we start working on our relationship with Him, allowing bits of His nature to rub off on us, we notice that the gap between our brokenness and His perfection begins, ever so slightly, to narrow. In short, we begin to get healed. Part of being the friend of God is to take up His offers of healing. Like a parent with a baby, He steadies us on our feet, getting us ready to walk. It's true; we are never going to be perfect this side of heaven, but turning Him down is not an option. God has both the power and the desire to heal us—not just our skin and bone, but our hearts and minds too. As we learn to lean on Him more, we tap into a source of incredible power.

Jesus knew that He was on the earth for a purpose. Just after we read about His baptism in the Holy Spirit, we hear what happened when He went into His local synagogue one Sabbath. He stood up to read and was handed the scroll of the prophet Isaiah. Unrolling it, He found the place where it is written:

> The Spirit of the Lord is on me, because he has anointed me to preach good news to the poor. He has sent me to proclaim freedom for the prisoners and recovery of sight for the blind, to release the oppressed, to proclaim the year of the Lord's favor (Luke 4:18-19).

Jesus then rolled up the scroll, gave it back it to the attendant and sat down. At this point, every eye was watching Him. Was the son of a carpenter seriously claiming that He was the *Great Hope* for the whole nation? Then came Jesus' answer: "Today this scripture is fulfilled in your hearing" (v. 21).

What Jesus Showed

Throughout His life, Jesus showed both the importance of relying on the Holy Spirit and the effectiveness of praying for healing. After He was thrown out of Nazareth, we follow His life through the Gospels and see that He was right to read this passage from Isaiah. The Spirit of the Lord was on Him, and He did have power. He preached good news to the prostitutes and the tax collectors, to the publicans and the sinners. He spent time with the outcasts, telling them that one day they would be first in the kingdom of heaven. He gave blind people back their sight. Some were physically blind, while others were spiritually blind. Those who had been prisoners of their emotions could once again feel the sun on their face. Jesus came down to Earth and brought with Him the biggest goodie bag ever seen by man. Regardless of whether people deserved His blessings, He traveled around and spread the healing good and thick. Jesus had such compassion, such love for the people that He couldn't help it; to heal was the most natural thing in the world for Him.

The fact that the area was bursting with former cripples who could now walk, men who were once blind but could now see, and former lepers who were clean again was a sign that the kingdom of God was real and accessible. Hearing of all those miracles opened peoples' eyes, and the word began to spread. As well as showing God's love, healing people showed that God was alive.

The healing didn't stop when Jesus left us. He told the disciples that they were to watch out for the Holy Spirit who would guide them, comfort them and help them take the message to the rest of the world. At Pentecost, the Spirit showed up and made quite an impression (see Acts 2). The disciples went on to preach and do good deeds and works by healing the sick, casting out demons and raising the dead. The lives they lived were modeled on what they had seen while Jesus was on the earth.

One day Peter and John were going up to the temple at the time of prayer—at three in the afternoon. Now a man crippled from birth was being carried to the temple gate called Beautiful, where he was put every day to beg from those going into the temple courts. When he saw Peter and John about to enter, he asked them for money. Peter looked straight at him, as did John. Then Peter said, "Look at us!" So the man gave them his attention, expecting to get something from them.

Then Peter said, "Silver or gold I do not have, but what I have I give you. In the name of Jesus Christ of Nazareth, walk." Taking him by the right hand, he helped him up, and instantly the man's feet and ankles became strong. He jumped to his feet and began to walk. Then he went with them into the temple courts, walking and jumping, and praising God. When all the people saw him walking and praising God, they recognized him as the same man who used to sit begging at the temple gate called Beautiful, and they were filled with wonder and amazement at what had happened to him (Acts 3:1-10).

The good stuff didn't die with the Early Christians either. Today we have just as much a job to do as they did, sharing the same tools. The Bible is more than a history book. The apostles took the stories of how Jesus went about His business as blueprints for their own behavior, and it is still the same for us today. Our friends and society need to know that God is alive and loving, and should we choose to accept our mission to tell them about Christ, we can set out on that mission fully equipped. The Spirit of the Lord is still here with His people; the Church is still setting the captives free and binding up the brokenhearted. Today God is saying to His people, "I want to use all of you to do My work."

Early Days

I was in a strange state when I arrived at Saint Andrew's Chorleywood. I was bruised and hurt, tired of feeling like a featherweight sparring partner for some particularly vicious heavyweights. I used to sit at the back of the church, soaking up the vibes as God mingled with His people. At the end of each service, there were opportunities for people who wanted prayer to go up to the front and have members of the ministry team pray for them. At first I just watched to see which prayer team members were consistently getting results in the healing department. I watched the people being prayed for and discovered that, on the whole, good things seemed to happen. Often at the start of the following week's service, people would stand up and say what had happened to them and how God had worked in them.

Having devised a particularly elaborate scoring system (based on numbers of falling-overs, weepings, shakings and shoutings), I decided which team member was a healing pro and headed for him at the end of one particular service. This was a particularly busy evening, and in the confusion a woman with swollen ankles nabbed the professional pray-er. I was left with a second-rate team member—not quite what I had hoped for, but I felt generous so I let him carry on. That night, I met God and was filled by His Spirit. Something happened in me; something was reignited.

After that I went up for prayer regularly, until I panicked, thinking that people might start to think that I was one of *those* sorts of people who was always going up for prayer. Then after one service, the pastor stopped me as I was leaving. There was no way of escape, so I decided to face up to the inevitable charge of being *one of those sorts of people.* But to my surprise he didn't give me a slap but instead asked me to join the ministry team. I said yes before he could find out that I was as unspiritual as a paper hole-puncher and change his mind.

At the beginning I was put with someone who was more experienced and who knew what to say. I acted as the assistant and worked out that if nothing else, I could at least try to catch people if they fell down. I soon became expert in a number of radical techniques, not least of which were the Sidewinder, the Back Flip and the Double Whammy.

I saw God minister to people when we prayed, but deep down I really thought that it was because of the other person's prayers and not mine. At times I would feel down, but it all changed in an instant. It was mid-June, and a number of visitors had turned up at the church. So many people came forward that I had to pray with someone on my own. A sudden terror hit me. I pleaded with God to give me someone with a mild headache, but instead I ended up with a bloke in his thirties. I asked him what his problem was.

"Well, there are two things," he said. "I've had a problem in my lower back for a number of years, and I've also been suffering from depression. That's it really."

My mind crashed with panic . . . fear . . . help . . . run away . . . lie . . .

"Let's have a bash at the depression, shall we?" I said after a few minutes had passed.

I prayed the first thing that came into my head: "Lord, please would You come and heal his depression?" I waited (because that's what they told us to do) and tried to work out some decent excuses for why he would still feel depressed, when he opened his eyes and said, "That was amazing. It just feels like it's lifted. I feel like I'm floating on air."

"Really?" I said. I could hardly believe it. I thought it might be good to try praying for his back, so I put my hand on his back and asked the Lord to heal that too. After a while he opened his eyes and thanked me for my prayers. I figured the back wasn't healed, but a 50 percent success rate wasn't bad for a beginner.

Then he came running up to me, jumping about wildly, showing me how his back had been completely healed. I left the church walking on air. I knew then that I was holy, spiritual and the possessor of a rare healing ministry. I planned my first book—it would be called *Mike Pilavachi: Man of Miracles*. I couldn't wait for the next Sunday to come so that I could pray for someone again. Perhaps we should go to the cemetery.

The next Sunday came and I prayed for someone. This time though nothing much appeared to happen. I prayed harder than ever before but still nothing happened. I was puzzled and asked God why, when I expected nothing, He did so much the week before, but when I was ready to see miracles this week I might as well have been praying to a gnome. Then the classic verse from Proverbs 3:34, James 4:6 and 1 Peter 5:5 came into my mind again: "God opposes the proud but gives grace to the humble." I realized that I was getting proud and missing the point of it all. It was never supposed to be about me having a great ministry or even having a great time. At the end of the day it's all about Him, about His generosity, His grace and His ability to heal.

How Do You Pray for Healing?

So, having figured out that praying for people is a good thing to do, and having got clear on just how much of an ego trip it can be for us, we come to the nuts and bolts of it and ask, "How?" First, to pray for healing is not to pray a 2,000-word essay on the root causes of society's fall from grace. Nor is it to shout so loud and propel so much saliva into the person's face that they break down in tears. Here's what you can do:

1. Ask the person what he or she wants prayer for. At this stage, you aren't after a full-on medical diagnosis complete with case notes, just a rough idea of what's wrong. If possible, get that person to show you what's wrong, because afterwards you'll have something against which to measure what God has done.

2. Tell the person to relax and that you're going to pray for him or her. It can help if that person has her or her eyes closed and places his or her hands out in front, as if to receive a present, which is exactly what is going to happen.

3. Invite the Holy Spirit. You can pray something like, "Lord Jesus, please send Your Holy Spirit now." We do this because we want God to do the healing, and Jesus

told us that the Holy Spirit would be more than just a little handy in this sort of situation. Having asked Him to come, it's time to wait.

4. After a while you may notice that the person starts to look more peaceful. Or he or she might just look the same. Either way, just wait.

5. And wait some more.

6. If we ask He will come, so it's important to wait for as long as it takes. Once the person looks more peaceful—or maybe has started to sway a little—you will want to pray some more. If it's a physical problem, you might want to pray something like, "Lord, I pray that you would heal this condition." You may feel that it is appropriate to say, "In the name of Jesus be healed." Alternately, you may just want to pray quietly or gently put your hand on the person's shoulder or (if it's not too personal) on whatever part of the body that needs healing. This also applies to praying for people's emotions. You can pray out loud if you feel that you have something to say, but at the end of the day, it's up to God. We're just helping the person to focus on Him.

7. Then you need to wait some more. Carry on asking God to heal, and thank Him if you think something's going on. Even if you're desperate to get home, it is vital that the person who has come for prayer leaves feeling loved

and valued. That means no laughing at the person, no talking about his or her dress sense to your mates, and no walking off to grab a coffee halfway through. When the person is good and ready, he or she will open his or her eyes and you can chat about what that person thought was going on.

8. At the end of it all, you might want to pray briefly again, thanking God for what He's done and asking Him to bless and keep on looking after the person. Often, things start in a ministry time but get finished days later, so it can be useful to suggest that the person keep on praying too, looking out for God doing things in him or her.

9. Don't ask for a tip.

Putting On a Good Show

Of course, what really doesn't matter in all of this is making it look good. As you can tell from my early experiences, trying to force the situation just doesn't work. The whole process may take a long time, or it may be over in a flash. The person may jump around or stand completely still. Whatever happens, there is no need to try to make something happen. When we ask the Lord to come, we are asking for a gift from the Lord, not some nonsense that we find floating around in the backwaters of our own minds. In Matthew 7:7 Jesus says that we should "ask and it will be given." So whenever we ask, we can leave it all up to Him.

Sometimes when we pray for someone to be filled with the Holy Spirit, hear God's voice for direction or be healed physically or emotionally, we may see certain things happen. There can sometimes be shaking, sometimes laughter. Sometimes the person might lie down on the floor. This won't always be the case, and we shouldn't encourage it, but when these things do happen, it's good, like smoke coming out of a chimney. It might be a sign that someone's home, but then again the person may have central heating and show no signs. Either way, it's what's going on inside that really counts. The goal is not the physical manifestation; the goal is that we meet with Jesus and give Him space and time to work on our lives. The goal is that, like Jesus and the apostles that followed Him, we let people know that God is both generous and alive.

Respect

We want to treat people with the dignity and respect that all children of God deserve. We have found at Soul Survivor and at other places that when we give the Holy Spirit the room to move, He often tackles some really deep hurts. As buried pain comes up to the surface, often people weep. The key to praying for someone in this situation is respect, both for the person—how would you feel if you were that person? Would it be better if you found somewhere more private to pray?— and for what God is doing. If there's that much emotion, use common sense and realize that God is probably at work. Keep encouraging the person to stick with what God is doing, and keep asking God to do whatever He wants.

How Do You Begin?

Praying for people alongside the Holy Spirit is like cooking: You can get all the books, listen to all the tapes and watch all the videos, but the only way to really learn is to do it. I found it helpful to first team up with someone more experienced. This way, if it's a member of the opposite sex, you can pray for anyone. But if you're on your own or are teamed up with someone of the same sex, it's generally a pretty good rule to pray only with someone who has the same equipment as you, otherwise things could get a little complicated.

God created us as well as the rest of the universe. Therefore it is obvious that we should ask Him to restore the bodies He has made, heal the hearts that He understands, and fill with His power the lives He created. Because of this, it is vital that we don't hype anything up but simply let the Holy Spirit come down. We need to exercise the gift of faith when we pray for others and trust that God knows what He's doing and will do something good. Because He is God, occasionally some of the ways He does things are hard to understand.

In 1 Corinthians 12:7-13, we find a list of some of the gifts of the spirit—one of which is the gift of healing (see v. 9). Who gets the gift of healing? Surprisingly, it is not the person doing the praying but the person who needs the healing. There is no such thing as a group of people who carry the gift of healing around in their pockets. None of us is so spiritual that we carry that gift with us wherever we go. Instead, we need to see ourselves as waiters and waitresses in a restaurant. When we pray for someone, we take his or her order and pass it on to the Chef. Only He can prepare the dish. We get to have the fun of being involved in delivering the dish to the diner. Ultimately, healing is something God does, not us.

Why Bother?

None of this is meant so that we can have a cozy life, sitting around on those long winter nights, adding the finishing touches to our near-perfect souls. As we learn to pray for one another in these ways in the Church, God is preparing us to pray for people out in the world. Most of the miraculous healings and deliverances that happened in the New Testament, both in the life of Jesus and in the Early Church, happened outside the synagogue. Instead of setting up an exclusive service for members only, Jesus took it out to the people. Let's practice this in the Church, but let's not forget to take it with us when we go outside the Church.

This might be making you feel uncomfortable. The idea of inviting people up to the front of the bus for deliverance might not be quite your cup of tea. The truth is that it's not mine either. What we can do is learn to pray for people in a normal way, without all the jargon and religion. Praying for someone who knows nothing of God or church has a maximum risk factor, and because of that, a massive potential for

God to do something great. Let's devote ourselves to learning how to pray for people outside the safety of the Church, just as Jesus did.

Many Christians think of the Holy Spirit as an "it." He is not an "it"; He is a person. When we think of God the Father, we understand the concept because most of us have fathers (however good or bad they are). When we think of Jesus, we imagine a person, whether we picture Him with long blond hair and a white nightie or (as in the *Jesus of Nazareth* film) with long black hair and a brown nightie. The Holy Spirit is much harder to visualize, but He is full of personality. The Early Church knew that the Holy Spirit was for real and trusted Him to do His thing. Knowing this will encourage us to trust in His power and not just our own.

Part 3:
GO

Chapter 10

WHY I LEFT HARROW
(A chapter about evangelism)

I want you to come on a journey with me. We are headed for North London in the mid-1970s. Big-haired rock is just about to give birth to a difficult baby named Punk, but our hero (me) remains completely oblivious to the noise. Instead, my "mono" is banging out the sounds of The Carpenters, Simon and Garfunkel and Max Bygrave's *Christmas Favorites* (there weren't many record shops out our way). Society is going through a tough period. Marriage doesn't seem to be worth much, but what is important is the business of enjoying your own life and making sure you have a good time.

As I seemed to be the only teenage Christian in the area of Harrow and Wealdstone, it made perfect sense that I appoint myself the *Last Hope for the Lost People Round Here*. Slim, tanned and enthusiastic, I was ready to take on the world, one postal district at a time. I spent weeks planning the offensive that would bring my neighbors to their knees. It was only a matter of a few hard days work and people would be throwing themselves at my feet as I walked to the garage, begging me to make personal introductions between them and God. I had found my weapon in a little-known bookshop; small, round and to the point, the solution was perfectly simple: stickers.

At the time, Coca-Cola was forcing its way into the English population's subconscious with the slogan "Coke—it's the real thing." The stickers I had were an exact copy, except for the fact that the word "Coke" was replaced with the name "Jesus." Perhaps the manufacturers had been in a rush, as they seemed to have forgotten to change the "it's" to "He's," which meant the stickers were a bit confusing, but I was sure that people would get the idea. I bought all the stickers they had and spent the next two nights applying them to every available surface: lampposts, cars, shop windows, coin slots on collection boxes, even the occasional dog. By the end, I had stuck up 743 of these stickers. I sat back and waited for the revival to break out. If 20 people saw each sticker per day, I was sure that by tea time the streets would be full of people weeping and wailing, ready for the short sermon that I had prepared.

It was a week later that I returned to the Christian bookshop. Nobody had approached me directly since my sticker campaign, although a couple of dogs did seem to be hanging around my house a bit more than usual. I was just about to ask the assistant for some more supplies when I heard her tell another customer about a particular problem that she was encountering. I moved closer.

"It's terrible—we've had so many calls from people who are totally irate about these stickers. It's such a bad witness and I've been going round scraping them off wherever I can." I left the shop.

The Best Way to Evangelize

Christians have been arguing for years about the best way to evangelize. A whole bunch of Christians (let's call them "conservative evangelicals") have said that the way to do it is to preach it. For them nothing else quite cuts the mustard like getting up and proclaiming the good news with a clear voice. They point to Jesus as an example of preaching leading to conversions and take Paul's trips as proof that hearing the Word is the best way for someone to become a Christian.

We have another group in the Church (we might call them the "social gospelers") who say that the thing that counts is the way we live—that the gospel is best preached through our deeds. They say that people are tired of words, that what they want is action. The Gospels, they say, are full of references to what Jesus did as well as to what He said, and it is the things He did that caught people's attention. These people say that the gospel that is waiting to be heard is actually a gospel that can be seen—a gospel that makes a difference to peoples' lives. We've got to build houses, care for the Third World, get involved in the environment and so on. They quote the widely known phrase often attributed to Saint Francis of Assisi: "Go into all the world and preach the gospel. If necessary, use words."

What really matters to the third group (the "charismatics") are signs and wonders—this is the idea that when people see, they believe. The charismatics point to the Scriptures and say that what actually caught peoples' attention were the miracles, the supernatural things. When Jesus healed, people listened; when He prophesied, they were all ears. Today, say the charismatics, people want to see, feel and touch the power of God, not just to hear about it.

Which one of these three is the right opinion? The answer, I believe, is all of them; the way to get the gospel out onto the streets is through a combination of each of the three. Jesus gave us a gospel to proclaim through *words*, *works* and *wonders*, and when we miss out one or two of them, the power of the gospel is never as strong. Jesus proclaimed the gospel in the things He said. If we do not proclaim it, people will not know. He also lived it in the way He cared for people, in the way He sided with the marginalized—He spent time with the publicans and the sinners and the prostitutes and the tax collectors and those rejected by polite society. He had a ministry of power; He did miracles; He healed and changed lives. In the Acts of the apostles, we see the same thing, the three ingredients of communicating the gospel coming together to make one big evangelism pie. We might like a little more of one taste than another, but the pie just won't be a pie unless we have each ingredient represented. The trouble with my sticker ministry was that it contained none of the above; as a pie, it sucked.

Early Experiences in Watford

In between the stickers and today, there have been plenty of mistakes, but by 1993, when 11 of us decided to set up a new church in Watford, we had gone through the worst of it. When we started Soul Survivor Watford, we all met in someone's living room. Looking around at the other 10, I panicked, totally unconvinced that God could do anything at all through them (as for myself, well, I knew the ground-breaking foul-ups I was capable of). We found that in the early days, the thing that we needed to concentrate on was not the preaching of the gospel with words or even signs and wonders, but the simple work of making friendships. Why should people be bothered to hear what we had to say if they didn't know us?

Soon after we started, two young guys, Dave and Liam, turned up. Both had long greasy hair and questionable personal hygiene—they were a nightmare. Dave had been thrown out of his house by his parents because he'd tried to set fire to it. Social Services had placed him with a Christian family whose sons had started coming to our little church. Dave and Liam were into everything that we weren't—drugs, drinking, fighting—and I was convinced that it was the very worst state of affairs for us to be in.

At first, both guys started coming to our social meetings. One of the early turning points was when we had a social evening with a curry dinner and a video. Dave challenged me to an eating competition—I have never consciously turned down a food-related challenge. I nearly died and he beat me hands down. He was so happy that I decided not to ask him to leave, and actually, it was this sort of thing that helped us become good friends.

As well as eating, we used to meet to worship, pray and listen to God. I remember one Wednesday evening looking around and seeing everybody deep in worship, but Dave had disappeared from sight. I first thought that he had finally become bored of it all, but I went to look for him just in case. I found him sitting on the floor behind the sofa with his head down. He was crying, so I asked what was wrong. "All this stuff about Jesus," he said, "it's really true, isn't it?" He gave his life to Jesus there and then, but none of it would have happened if he hadn't grown to trust and like us.

We Christians have a phrase that we quite like. It is that *Jesus is the answer.* There are plenty of non-Christians out there who quite rightly reply, "But what's the question?" We are trying to give answers to questions that aren't even being asked. It ought to be a natural by-product of our friendship with people who don't know Jesus that they begin to ask about Jesus. It should come from within rather than being forced down their throats by our impatience.

We started an outreach event called Dregs Café, which we hoped would give us an opportunity to make friends with people. This wasn't to be done in a patronizing way; we genuinely wanted to develop good relationships. We decided that we would never preach at them and that we would only talk about God if they brought the subject up. Mostly we danced, played cards, ate and drank and just had a laugh together. People started coming from the different schools in Watford, and the first thing many of them said was that they liked Dregs because people were nice.

Over time, it was amazing to see lasting friendships develop and a number of people come to know Jesus, simply because they first came to know us. We have this little saying that we've stolen from somewhere (but we can't remember where we've taken it from) that goes like this: *The order is belonging, believing, behaving.* Traditionally, the Church has said to people that if people want to belong, they must *behave* themselves. A stranger to church must adjust to the way we do church, standing up at the correct times, sitting down when required. What the rest of the congregation reads out, the stranger has to read out as well, and he or she certainly doesn't smoke during the sermon or use the church bulletin to make paper airplanes. Once the behavior thing has been sorted out and the stranger can imitate the rest of the church, then he or she can stay long enough to hear the gospel preached and get round to *believing*. Only once that person believes will we baptize him or her, sing a cheesy little song about how welcome that person is and proclaim that he or she finally *belongs*.

Call me Mr. Cynical, but I would suggest that Jesus did it the other way around. When He called the disciples to Himself, He called them to *belong* to Him, to be together and be a family. Their *believing* then came in stages; for some of them, to leave their nets and follow Jesus must have meant some kind of belief, but we only have to look at Thomas to see a man who took his time to believe. Even after three years of Jesus' company, he still demanded to see the nail marks in Jesus' hands and touch the side of His resurrected body. John 20:9 says that even at the end, the disciples still did not understand from Scripture that Jesus had to rise from the dead. *Duh!*

As for their *behavior*, that also took some time to sort out. James and John were nicknamed the "sons of thunder" (see Mark 3:1), not because of their high-fiber diets, but because they could never control their tempers. Peter was always putting his foot in his mouth; and Judas betrayed Jesus. Even in the garden of Gethsemane when Jesus was in His very last hours, out of 12 disciples, one betrayed him, 10 ran away and one stayed long enough to tell three lies before he ran too. Great behavior. The *belonging* most definitely came first and was then followed by the *believing*, which came a long way before their *behavior* began to get better.

We need to make space in the Church for our friends so that they know they belong. At Soul Survivor Watford, there were quite a few who found that the transition from going to the Dregs Café to coming along to church wasn't very difficult. They already knew us and we had become friends.

Probably the Best Evangelism in the World

It seems pretty clear that the best evangelism comes out of friendship, because, as the saying goes, the only Bible some people will read is you. But we wanted more than just the friendship; we wanted people to have a chance to meet Jesus. Just relying on preaching the gospel through our works would have left us unsatisfied. By inviting them along to church, they had a chance to have the gospel shown to them, not only through the words of the talk and the songs, but also through the signs and wonders of a full-on ministry session.

After Dregs had been going for a while and people were taking us up on our offers of a night out at church, we started to think that the whole system was a pretty good way of showing our new friends that we weren't a group of sad weirdos. Then came the whole Toronto revival thing. Suddenly our meetings were interrupted by a repertoire of animal impressions that would have had Old MacDonald calling up for some farm help. God was doing something great in the hearts of His people, but it all seemed to be happening in very bizarre ways. The plan of singing a little worship followed by a very good talk from a wonderful and well-known preacher leading to positive responses to the gospel from the new folks was, I thought, ruined. "Lord," I prayed, "this is wonderful, but not here." The Lord and I had a bit of a discussion about the whole thing, and at the end we came to an agreement that since He was God and I wasn't, we'd try it His way first. To my amazement, the people who found it least difficult were the non-Christians, whereas it was mostly some of the Christians who found the weirder stuff difficult.

One day, five people arrived together at the church for the first time. They had been to Dregs a few times and said that they wanted to come along on a Sunday. Of all the people we had met, I was convinced that these were the ones who were going to leave the minute the service started. I lost sight of them for a bit but found them toward the end of the meeting. Each one was lying face down on the floor. I asked one of the girls what was going on. "I dunno," she replied helpfully. Digging a bit deeper, I asked whether or not it was a *good dunno* or a *bad dunno*. She said it was a good one.

"Do you know that it's Jesus?" I asked.

"I think so," she said.

I asked her if she had asked Him into her life and she said she hadn't.

"Would you like to do it now?"

"Yes," she said.

So we clinched the deal there and then.

Back Down to Earth

A couple of weeks later, a youth leader friend of mine, Silas, came up to see how Dregs was going. To be honest, I was showing off my little trophies, all those new Christians, which was an awful thing to do. We got to one of the five that had wound up on the floor a couple of weeks back, and I asked her to tell Silas the story of how she became a Christian. Becky said that when she turned up at church she was an atheist, going along just to be with her friends. "Then the Holy Spirit came on me and I fell down." She obviously needed some help with this testimony thing, so I reminded her that she had missed the part about how in the worship time she had sensed something wonderful. That was then followed by the sermon, which explained Christianity so well that she decided to give her life to Jesus, and then the Holy Spirit came and she fell down.

"No," she interrupted. "I went down an atheist and came up a Christian."

In Becky's case, the wonders and the works worked very closely together. It was the power of God at work that convinced her, and she wouldn't have come along if she didn't have friends there. But at the same time, there had to be a place for explaining what was happening as well as what the Cross meant to her. Words, works and wonders need to exist together. We need to be flexible in our approach to each person, but at the same time make sure that we value each way of expressing the gospel. When we miss out on one, we take away from the fullness of the message of the Cross.

There have been many studies into the growth of churches, all of which have ended up agreeing on the same point: that we appeal to those people who are most like us. The thing about friendship evangelism is that the friendship needs to be genuine. When Dregs was going on, I wasn't the first person up leading the moves for when the good song came on, nor was I comparing stunts with the skaters outside. Dregs attracted people who were like most of the people in our church.

The key to it all is to love people for who they are, not for another notch on your conversions chart. People can smell a rat without too much trouble. We had to reach a point where we were going to love and care for people whether they made a response or not. We were also never going to hide the fact that we would love for them to respond to Jesus because we believe that Christianity is a fantastic, life-changing thing.

Reading this might give you the impression that everybody who walked through the doors of the Dregs Café ended up on their knees at the foot of the Cross. Unfortunately, that didn't always happen. The majority of people became our friends and left it at that. We had one guy who came all the time but who never made a commitment. While we knew there was more for him in Jesus, we had to leave it to him, happy that friendship is a valid way of expressing God's love. We are called to love people as God loves them: unconditionally. Our primary calling is to care for people—that's where the works of social action come in. We serve the poor because we love God.

We Christians are supposed to be the nicest people around, the most generous with our time and money. Our friendships must be because God calls us to be friends with people, to be good and caring people. We are called to proclaim the gospel with our words and our lives and with the power of God, modeling ourselves on the life of Jesus.

Postscript—Back to Harrow

As I walked home from the bookshop (the one with the stickers), I felt sick inside as I remembered the shop assistant's thoughts about my sticker idea. It was then that I thought of a new evangelism strategy. I would open the phonebook to a random page, pick and dial a number and play some worship down the phone, immediately bringing the listener to his or her knees. The only trouble was that the closest thing I had to worship music was Max Bygrave's version of "The Holly and the Ivy." But it was worth a shot.

Chapter 11

GO
(Another chapter about evangelism)

> Then the eleven disciples went to Galilee, to the mountain
> where Jesus had told them to go. When they saw him, they
> worshiped him; but some doubted. Then Jesus came to them
> and said, "All authority in heaven and on earth has been
> given to me. Therefore go and make disciples of all nations,
> baptizing them in the name of the Father and of the Son and
> of the Holy Spirit, and teaching them to obey everything I
> have commanded you. And surely I am with you always, to
> the very end of the age" (Matt. 28:16-20).

This is an account of the last words that Jesus spoke to His
disciples before He returned to heaven. Today the Great Commission is as powerful and relevant to us as it was to Jesus'
audience 2,000 years ago. In fact, we exist as Christians partly

because of the extent to which the group of 12 took Jesus' command seriously. Like a line of dominoes, each generation inherits parts of the previous generation's character and reaps the rewards of the previous generation's work. If we want to see the gospel interacting on a greater level with the rest of the world, the responsibility lies with us. If we squander our chance to follow Jesus' simple instruction, we not only risk opportunities today, but we also erase them for tomorrow.

To live the life means to spend time in worship of the King, to allow time and space for the Holy Spirit to heal and empower us; but it will be meaningless if we stand with boots of lead, immovable and apathetic. When the passion witnessed in the meeting is fused with action outside, our words have integrity and our deeds have power. We need to learn to give away what we've received.

Two Breakthroughs

I recently spent a few months getting increasingly excited and frustrated about the whole "go" concept (excited because I wanted to do it, frustrated because I had built up my life without doing it). This particular time of change was marked by two separate events.

The first happened at Spring Harvest 1997. Matt Redman and I met up with the World Wide Message Tribe for a bit of discussion. Neither of us anticipated what would happen during those two hours. God ambushed us. As we all talked about what our hopes were for the future, each one of us felt that the Lord was doing something inside. We all realized again how much God has given us and that the only response is to get our hands dirty. When we understand that God doesn't give us gifts so that we can let them grow old and stale, then we look at our gifts and talents in a totally different way. It is no longer possible to stay within our comfort zones. God is infinitely practical and makes His power available where the need is greatest. I left that meeting a changed man.

The second event could not have been more different. Instead of being surrounded by people, I was alone. Instead of God brewing up an intense and tangible atmosphere over an afternoon, I spent time quietly thinking about things and eating pizza. While staying at a friend's home in Dorset, I read through the Acts of the apostles. As I read, I asked God what the differences were between the first church and our church. I was amazed at the answer. This must have been the fiftieth time I had read the book, and it was only then that I felt as though I really understood. The answer was this: The difference between the first church and ours lay not in their power encounters with the Holy Spirit or in their theological education, it lay in their obedience to the command to go and tell others about Him.

Obeying the command was their main priority, and they were sure to follow through when things were tough as well as when they were easy. When they were met with persecution, they went out to the lost with as much eagerness as when their message was met with thanks and joy. It all kicked off at Pentecost when they preached the gospel for the first time—assisted by the Holy Spirit. For a first attempt, the boys didn't do too badly, notching up 3,000 converts to Christianity (see Acts 2:41). If it had been me, I would have demanded a few warm-up gigs before I risked it in front of that many people, but the apostles knew that they were to do what Jesus had told them, so out they went.

Afterward, Peter and John were on their way to the Temple when they met a beggar. Those of you who paid attention in previous chapters will remember their reply: "Silver or gold I do not have, but what I have I give you. In the name of Jesus Christ of Nazareth, walk" (Acts 3:6). The beggar did what he was told and left that place walking and jumping, praising God for what He had done.

Not surprisingly, the Pharisees and the teachers of the Law were not happy about all this, and they had Peter and John arrested. The apostles were then threatened and commanded to quit preaching the gospel (see Acts 4:2-5,18). Peter and John returned to the others and got on with praying about the rather sticky situation. It is at this point that they blow a Christian like myself out of the water. Instead of adopting a Pilavachiesque technique like "Oh Lord, please help us because we're in trouble," they turned to the Lord and asked for boldness to proclaim so that they could get right back out there and kick butt. As they prayed, the Holy Spirit came and filled them. God's presence was so real that even the walls shook (see Acts 4:29-31).

Then there was a guy named Steven. He proclaimed Jesus so frequently and with such passion that the authorities had him stoned to death. He was the first Christian martyr and his death set off an increase in the hostilities against the Early Christians (see Acts 6:8–8:3). They were soon scattered all over the surrounding area, having fled from Jerusalem. On arrival in locations throughout Judea and Samaria, instead of laying low and trying not to get themselves killed, the apostles started, once again, to heal, teach and spend time with people (see Acts 8:4-8). They took His command seriously and turned the world upside down.

As I read the book of Acts, I had to repent of something I have often said. I used to believe that the Acts of the apostles should be called the Acts of the Holy Spirit, because it was all about the work of the Holy Spirit. I don't think that anymore; these events should be called the Acts of the apostles because the apostles acted. They did something; they made a difference, and I believe God is telling us today to go and make a difference in whatever way, big or small. The importance does not depend on the number of people who witness our activity but on the very fact that we obey our calling. It is about time that we take this seriously and act like those disciples who we claim to admire.

Looking for a Blessing

I discovered long ago that revival does not come when we go across the ocean to *receive* a blessing, as some have done in recent years, it comes when we go across the street to *be* a blessing. The salvation of our nations lies, not surprisingly, in our own hands. If we choose to value our neighbors by offering them a full range of practical expressions of the gospel, the chances are that they will be a lot more inclined to hear what we have to say than if we show them our slides from the latest overseas location of blessing.

The Scriptures are full of exhortations for God's people to go, and at times I have been puzzled; bearing in mind that Jesus repeated Himself so often on the subject, what part of the command do we have a problem with? Is it the *G* or the *O*? Like much of our faith, the basis is very simple and is applicable to absolutely everybody.

Go with the Flow

At times, the outpouring of God's blessing has been likened to the river mentioned in Ezekiel 47. It is a great picture of a river that flows out from the altar (the place of sacrifice, the cross). After a while the water is ankle deep, then knee deep, then up to the waist and then finally it is over the head. At that point it is impossible to walk; you need to swim in the river. The river symbolizes the Spirit of God and can be taken as an encouragement not just to paddle in God's spirit or to wade, but to go all the way and give in to the power of God in our lives. The important question is, Where is the river going? We need to allow God's Spirit to take us where He wants us to go, giving over control of our lives to Him.

God wants to be the boss of His people. He wants more than our attendance at meetings; He wants our whole lives. Ezekiel 47 tells us that the river was going to the sea to make the salt waters fresh. It was going out into the world, and where the river flowed, there would be lots of fish and fruit trees growing along the shore. In the Bible, fish symbolize non-Christians, which is why Jesus told Peter and Andrew that He would make them fishers of men (see Matt. 4:19).

If we also want to see life reinjected into the world, we need to follow the river and find the fish.

The choice to stay within the Church will inevitably lead to a misty-eyed nostalgia for the glory days. Whatever happened to those days? we will ask ourselves. The answer will be short and simple: The Spirit of God moved out into the world and we Christian muppets have stayed in the Church.

How Do We Go?

Jesus announced the beginning of His ministry with the words "The Spirit of the Lord is on me, because he has anointed me to preach good news to the poor. He has sent me to proclaim freedom for the prisoners and recovery of sight for the blind, to release the oppressed, to proclaim the year of the Lord's favor" (Luke 4:18-19).

This was Jesus' manifesto. He came to preach the good news of forgiveness and salvation, proclaim freedom and bring healing and release from oppression. He came to bring justice. This good news was for the poor, not simply the poor in Spirit, but also the financially and materially poor. The freedom was for those unjustly imprisoned; the release was for those who were under the yoke of oppression. The year of the Lord's favor was the time when debts were canceled and slaves were set free.

Jesus did not simply proclaim this good news; He *was* the good news. He didn't stop at sympathizing with the poor and oppressed; He became one of them. Jesus was God becoming poor. He spent time with the publicans and sinners and treated them gently while He treated the Pharisees and teachers of the Law harshly.

We must imitate Jesus' actions when He talked to the Samaritan woman at the well in John 4. She was a social outcast and Jesus had plenty of time for her. So must we.

There is a chance that this strikes a chord with you but that you are left feeling confused and unsure about the very nature of *going*—just how, you might wonder, is it done? Fortunately, there is no hierarchy here; we all have a chance to express God to others—it is not something that we leave to the evangelists. For every person for whom God is a stranger, there is an endless combination of words, works and wonders that he or she will find relevant. The key to loving our neighbors (or those we have contact with), the starting block on which all else is built, is friendship. Without genuine friendship our words are distant, our works are hollow and the wonders don't have much to work through. We can start with our families. Sometimes it seems that it would be easier to go to Australia and evangelize than to stay home and live the Christian life among those people who know us best and who see us at our worst.

The poor are all around us. Whether their poverty is defined by finance, relationship, health or faith, there are many out there. In the same way, we can give via our wallet, our time, our energy or our skills. From a random act of kindness to a full-on regular commitment, God is ready to put our actions to use.

A group of people on our training course noticed that the bus stop opposite their house regularly had elderly people waiting at it in the cold. They decided to take some chairs out for the elderly people to sit on and some coffee for them to drink. There was no ulterior motive—they didn't make the old biddies listen to a talk on the seven spiritual laws in return for the favor—they were simply doing what they (and we) have been told to do. After all, we Christians are supposed to be the nicest, most generous, most considerate people on the face of the earth.

Another bunch decided one evening that they would go down the road and wash people's cars. They didn't accept any money and didn't draw parallels between the cleansing nature of the sponge and the water and the redeeming power of the Cross and the Son. It was just a nice thing to do, so they did it.

Part of belonging to the Western culture means that we also have a responsibility to look out for those who have inherited less than us by chance of birth. Organizations like Tear Fund, Toy Box or Amnesty International make it easy to get involved and produce detailed information on their projects. I once heard of a Christian who had refused to sign a petition to wipe out Third World debt because he did not feel that the Lord had called him to it. If his reason for refusing had been political, I would have felt differently, but as it was, the news made me sad. The truth is that we have been called; it is all there in black and white, the *G* and the *O*, the Great Commission, the call to set the captives free and be good news to the poor. There is no need to wait—some of us have been waiting for too long already. Our time on Earth is not a practice run—it is the real thing and the only chance we will ever get to be a light in the darkness. We do not have the luxury of saying no to God.

My prayer is that we are immersed in the power, love and glory of Jesus and that it has the same effect on us that it had on the apostles. I pray that we might be missionaries in our homes, in our schools, in our places of work, in our community and in our nation. We need to care for our cities and our world, and that care needs to be expressed in very practical ways.

I heard a story of an American man who decided to experiment with random acts of kindness. Whenever he arrived at a tollbooth, he would give twice the fee he owed and tell the attendant that he was paying for the car behind. The toll attendant assumed that he was traveling in a convoy and was paying for his friend rather than a complete stranger. He loved watching in his rear view mirror as the toll attendant tried to explain to a confused motorist why this guy had paid for him.

When a group of us were in South Africa, I shared this as an example in a talk, and the very next day we were driving around and actually came to a tollbooth. A wonderful friend suggested that I take a page out of my own book and pay for the guy behind us. I tried to explain the difference between using an example in a talk and actually doing it, but the poor fool just couldn't grasp it. Eventually I gave in and gave the attendant twice the fee, telling him that it was also for the next car. As we drove away, I slowed down and I looked in the rearview mirror. We all got excited because our follower seemed to be a particularly suspicious one and took quite some convincing that we were for real. As they left, I went even slower so that we could all wave as they went past. They waved at us and mouthed, "Thank you." I felt like a true spiritual hero.

A few days later we did it again, but this time the person who was lucky enough to be behind us didn't even look at us as he passed. I wanted to chase him down and give him a slap. Then I remembered that the point was to be like Jesus, not to give my ego a boost. Jesus often showed love to those who ignored Him, and if we are honest, we all spend a fair bit of time taking whatever He gives us without saying "thanks."

While reading this book, you may have spotted a couple of references to Mother Teresa. I am quite a fan of her life, yet like all good role models, hearing about things she said and did often leaves me feeling uneasy. I flinch as her sacrificial life highlights my own selfishness. Somebody once asked why she bothered doing what she did, bearing in mind that all the people she helped could only ever be a drop in the ocean. "This is true," she replied, "but the ocean is made up of many drops."[1]

Nothing we do for Jesus in the world is insignificant; God's ocean is made up of many drops, and like the hairs on our heads, each one is seen and known (see Matt. 10:30). Whatever you do, God wants to empower you, to help you do it again and again.

Let's read again the story that Jesus told about judgment:

Then the King will say to those on his right, "Come, you who are blessed by my Father; take your inheritance, the kingdom prepared for you since the creation of the world. For I was hungry and you gave me something to eat, I was thirsty and you gave me something to drink, I was a stranger and you invited me in, I needed clothes and you clothed me,

I was sick and you looked after me, I was in prison and you came to visit me." Then the righteous will answer him, "Lord, when did we see you hungry and feed you, or thirsty and give you something to drink? When did we see you a stranger and invite you in, or needing clothes and clothe you? When did we see you sick or in prison and go to visit you?" The King will reply, "I tell you the truth, whatever you did for one of these brothers of mine, you did for me" (Matt. 25:34-40).

We cannot divorce worship and justice; the Bible shows them glued together. The songs we sing must result in a change in the lives we live. For those who are unsure, it is worship to feed the hungry; it is worship to clothe the naked; it is worship to bless the homeless and to give them a home. All this is worship because Jesus said that when we do something for one of the lowest, we do something for one of the highest. Can we see Jesus out in the world beyond the Church? Can we bless Him and worship Him with our lives and not just with our words? This is a challenge, and a hard one at that. Agreeing to go does not guarantee a sugar-sweet passage through life, yet this is our time, our one chance to do it right. We might be praying for revival—a good thing—but let's live it out; let's take the gospel of Jesus to our broken and hurting world.

Note

1. Mother Teresa, quoted in "Army Rallies Its Troops," *British Broadcasting Corporation (BBC)*, March 11, 2005. http://www.bbc.co.uk/threecounties/con tent/articles/2005/03/08/heather_south_africa_visit_feature.shtml (accessed October 2005).

Chapter 12

HOW FAR SHOULD WE GO?

(Being part of the culture)

Is Christianity going through an image crisis? Do we owe it to our children to take on the job of bringing Jesus into the next millennium with worldwide sponsorship deals, a funky new logo and His own brand of cola? Face it, 2,000 years is a long time for anybody to keep the same wardrobe. I don't care what others may say: Staffs, sandals and smocks have gone for good. Should the Church be like every other successful company, where the customer is king, to be enticed in whatever ways are necessary to get the sale?

Or perhaps you hold another opinion: Christians never had it so good as when they lined pews with burning coals, the services lasted 18 hours and you could always be guaranteed a good witch hunt at the end. Is it up to the Church to plough forward (regardless of what century the service was written in), providing onlookers with a fine example of tradition, history and a dignity long forgotten in these days of video gaming and interactivity?

This isn't going to surprise anyone, but I make my camp somewhere in the middle of these two opinions. They are both a bit right and a lot stupid, which is probably a fairly good description of most of us when it comes to the issue of bringing God and our culture together.

So How Culturally Relevant Should We Be?

This question has caused more sulks and splits within the Church than many others. At the heart it can be divided into two separate questions: Should the Church change its style to make it more accessible? Should the Church change its message to fill up the pews?

Jesus did tell us how to pray, but thankfully, He didn't mention anything about rainbow sweaters, pipe organs or songs about rowing boats. This doesn't mean that we can't have them in church; I'm just suggesting that trying things without them is not an offense punishable by death.

Jesus (the one on whose life we are basing our own) made sure that His audience understood what He said. That doesn't mean that He spoke v-e-r-y s-l-o-w-l-y, made sure He used His hands a lot, and always gave out printed notes afterwards. What Jesus did was talk about situations and issues that everyone had come across already. For example, the language in which Jesus spoke was Aramaic. If you were after a really pure version of Christianity, it might upset you that the first Christians dared to translate Jesus' words into Greek. Their reason for changing the language was that Aramaic was slipping down the charts, being replaced by Greek as the "in" language. Today, there is only one village on top of a hill somewhere in Syria that still speaks Aramaic. If the writers of the Bible hadn't changed the language from Aramaic to Greek, the gospel today would only be understood in that one village. The first disciples changed the packaging to fit the people.

Paul said, "I have become all things to all men so that by all possible means I might save some" (1 Cor. 9:22). This doesn't mean that he saw the gospel of Christ as a giant buffet, where each person ate whatever entrée suited his or her pleasure. Paul became all things to all people in the way he communicated. Like Jesus, he made sure that he was understood. Jesus communicated in a way that was culturally relevant to His day; He didn't tell stories because the audience was a bit slow, but because everybody used stories and parables as part of their normal conversations. When He said, "I am the bread of life" (John 6:35), it was because bread was the staple diet. When, at the last supper, He took the bread and the wine and blessed it, saying, "This is my body . . . this is my blood" (see Luke 22:19-20), He was holding their equivalent of a Big Mac and a Diet Coke.

Sheep and Fish

Jesus taught about sheep because He talked to lots of people who spent time around sheep. He spoke about fish because there were lots of people listening to Him who made their living from the sea. The subjects He chose were vital parts of His culture. Jesus also talked about taxes, landowners and wedding banquets, but when He spoke about these He was in Jerusalem—where the fishermen, shepherds and farmers would have been replaced with those who made their living in other ways. The parable of the net in Matthew 13 put across a similar message in the country as the parable of the wedding banquet in Matthew 22 did in the city. Jesus is the King of kings, Lord of lords and also, I would suggest, the Captain of communication. He picked His words carefully to have maximum impact, showing each person that His message was for him or her. Two thousand years later and society has changed beyond all recognition: The industrial and technological revolutions have brought us to a new place, with new needs, new hurts and new horizons. What do we Christians talk about? Sheep and fish.

It is important to understand the language of Scripture, to find out what it meant then and what it means now. There is something enlightening about exploring the culture in which Jesus lived, but we shouldn't confuse our study with our outreach. Part of talking about issues that relate to people's lives means that we hopefully become a genuine part of that culture, just as Jesus did when He was in rural as well as urban areas.

Get Off My Land

The danger for the Church has often been that we form our own church culture. It can become as much of a clique as a golf club, a local political party or the cool group in the playground. These days I think God is challenging His people to actually care for the world so much that we make ourselves accessible to it. The gospel—with its no-compromise message of morality, purity and forgiveness—is on its own an offense to the "Me" culture of today; God doesn't need us to be snotty and offensive on top of it. We owe it to God and to all His children to ask ourselves whether the way we do things leaves people confused and uninterested or interested and welcome. When people come to our churches, are they met with strange rituals and mumbled jargon or do they find us easy to understand? This may start you off thinking about traditional churches, but things are just as bad, if not worse, in some of our more modern churches. We have all manner of styles and practices that can seem bizarre to the outsider. If we are serious about following Jesus, we will be sure to follow His lead and be ready to take the message out to as many different people as possible.

I was recently talking to a fashion photographer and I asked her why, as a Christian, she was involved in an industry that seemingly contradicts so much of the gospel. She told me that it was what she felt called to do. She told me that through her work she has been able to treat people with more dignity and respect than they have been used to. She knew that she had been called to do her job well and found that Jesus was as relevant to the fashion culture as He was to those who sleep on the streets.

A guy in our church had an idea to set up a club in the middle of town, playing the sort of music that he loves (and the sort that I think is just too fast to do anything to). His reason was that it was his culture and he loved it.

A little while back we set up an after-school club in our warehouse. Three afternoons each week, about 30 children whose parents can't afford to pay for childcare come along and have time and energy devoted to them. The reason for this is simple: Jesus told us to get involved with our culture.

This is the beautiful thing about Christianity: High fashion, hyperactive eight-year-olds and drum and bass may not have a whole lot in common with each other, but God is so wide and so creative that He makes each one of us with different passions. The gospel is so powerful and good that it relates to everyone; it's not bound by culture. These are the best places from which to evangelize; follow an instinct or whatever excites and we meet like-minded people and can make friendships and talk about the gospel in ways that are relevant.

The Beat of a Different Drum

On the other hand, there are certain things about which we are meant to be countercultural. When the Early Christians translated Jesus' words from Aramaic, they changed the packaging, but they made sure they left the point intact. While Jesus changed the stories, He never deviated from the message He came to give. That message is a challenge to many aspects of culture: Instead of selfishness, it talks about generosity; instead of sexual freedom, it talks about purity; instead of death being a kind of nothingness, it talks about heaven and hell. Sometimes we are meant to be prophetic to the culture, not to be so absorbed in it that we are indistinguishable from it. On certain issues, we are supposed to speak out and speak up if something is wrong. The way we do this though is not by pointing the finger and condemning but by living a different life and showing that we care by getting involved.

Where there is greed in our culture, we need to live lives of incredible generosity. Where there is a high abortion rate, we need to be there to help single mothers. Where there is crime and vandalism, we need to train and equip people to support themselves with dignity. The Sermon on the Mount is the last word about living in culture: "Love your enemies, do good to those who hate you. Give, and it will be given to you. A good measure, pressed down, shaken together and running over, will be poured into your lap" (Luke 6:27,38). As Jesus said it then, it's still relevant today, and it still goes against the grain. That's what makes real Christianity attractive, because it's something totally unique; it's something beautiful and pure.

We've gone wrong in the past by presenting the gospel in a way that's totally alien to society, but we have matched the rest of society for greed, ambition and selfishness. Perhaps we have avoided saying the *F* word, or have managed to wrap ourselves up in tradition and religion and call it *being a good Christian*. The fact remains that we have missed the point.

We have to think long and hard about the areas in which we need to be relevant to people—we can't please all of them all the time—and we also need to put plenty of energy into working out what they need to know about Jesus. But some things don't change: Jesus did die on a cross; He did rise again; He did die for our sins. These truths can't change; they are the Christian message, but how we communicate that message needs to change for different cultures.

Chapter 13

WHERE SHOULD WE GO?
(What is your calling in life?)

I always used to think of myself as being like one of the kids from *Fame*, that T.V. show from the 1980s. Each episode of *Fame* began with Miss Lydia Grant sitting backward on an old chair, wearing excessively large leg warmers and banging her stick on the ground as she emphasized the creed that she imparted to all those deeply soulful pupils: "You want fame? Well fame costs, and here's where you start paying—in sweat." I always felt a rush of excitement as those who were younger and less well-endowed in the leg-warmer department opened their eyes wide and prepared to work like Trojans for the next 30 minutes toward the ultimate goal: fame.

My reasons for comparing myself with "the kids" may not be immediately obvious, but the truth must be known. My rush of emotion at the beginning of the show was not the result of my desire to land the lead role in a Broadway show; it was at the small thought that I too might do something great one day and do it for God. While Leeroy, Denise and Bruno had visions of landing themselves a big job with a fat paycheck, I was coming up with rough concepts for my Mike Pilavachi: Man of Faith World Tour.

In those days, I was generally a bit rough around the edges of my faith. While I meant well enough, when my enthusiasm met my inexperience, the consequences were often amusing. I thought that my goal was the Christian spotlight, and if I wanted it with as much single-minded passion as the Famesters, I would surely end up satisfied.

I later found out that I was wrong. I found this verse:

> Whatever you do, work at it with all your heart, as working for the Lord, not for men, since you know that you will receive an inheritance from the Lord as a reward (Col. 3:23-24).

This verse says it all to me. Many of us think that to work full-time for Christ means working full-time for the Church. I had wanted the glitz and the glamour of church work—a part of me had wanted people to look at me and think, *There goes Mike. He gets paid to be holy*, even though my heart was (kind of) in the right place. I genuinely thought that being a missionary was the only way to use your work life in a God-pleasing way. I had to wait from when I was 16 until I was 29 before I went into what I thought was full-time Christian work. Looking back, I'm convinced that I wasted those years. I was too busy waiting for the calling to come from Africa to realize that God was trying to use me in Harrow. Calling, I have since found out, is all about the present, and consequently wherever you are there is a call of God to do His will.

What Is Full-Time Christian Work?

My confusion started with a simple misunderstanding of the facts. What I thought was full-time Christian work can be described as full-time church work, because every Christian who is living as a disciple of Jesus is into full-time Christian work; when we belong to Him, everything we do belongs to Him—not only our money, but also our time. Whatever we do, we should see it as our calling; otherwise there is little point in us being there. The Church is full of people who feel stuck in a job to which they feel they have no calling; then they wait for the right job to come along. There really is no time like the present for knuckling down and doing things that please God's heart.

I feel slightly ashamed of myself when I think of how I wasted the first seven years of my secular employment. I was hired on a temporary contract and remained on one despite the fact that I was offered numerous chances to sign up for something a bit more permanent. My attitude to the job spread over in my attitude to the staff; *after all*, I thought, *I'll be in Africa before long, so it would be silly to develop any really deep friendships.* It was only in the last two years there that I found some sense and realized what a fool I'd been. I decided that my career was worthy of God and began to put in more effort. Soon after, I began to get promotions and got to know my colleagues on a deeper level than before. Then God stepped in.

I'm not sure whether it was divine punishment or humor, but this was about the time that God decided to finally offer me a chance to get involved in some full-time church work. What I had spent almost 12 years dreaming of, placing on a pedestal and considering to be sheer perfection was now a sacrifice. Giving up the job meant much more than escaping from the boredom of secular work. I did quit my job, but I know that those final two years helped me to mature. I'm also sure that had I decided to stay there, God would have used me and called me to express His nature in the middle of the office.

Widening the View

Sometimes, being at school, at college or in secular work is tough. When a range of issues that are totally alien to the Sunday service confront us, it can get difficult. While a job as seemingly mundane as putting out the chairs before the church meeting can easily be thought of as useful, the work of an accountant can be slightly harder to spiritualize. The secular worker is faced with all manner of internal questions about his or her job: Is it valid? Is it making a difference? How does it count in the grand scheme of things?

The problem here stems from a twisted view of what God wants. The reason for writing a chapter like this is to challenge the myth that if your employer doesn't incorporate a little fish in its logo, then your job can't be serving the Lord. Our value system has ignored relationship and preaching of the gospel, replacing it with the strange notion that the Church is a hospital, training ground and an employment agency too. Think for a minute about the model that Jesus gave us; it was all about relationship, all about living the life.

Being an accountant may not call upon the skills of biblical insight that will be required of a man or woman of the cloth, but if you line up the spiritual gifts, it's plain to see that they can be incorporated into any workplace.

Being a pastor goes beyond saying, "So how is your walk with the Lord, Gerald?" On a basic level, being a pastor is caring for people and encouraging their development—a fine description of a good colleague.

Evangelism can take many forms, but statistically most people get to know Jesus through friendship with a Christian. If you've managed to care for people and have encouraged their development, then you will have established a caring, attentive relationship, out of which either your colleagues will want to know about your faith or you can let them know bit by bit.

Our faith, the thing that we are living for, is more than capable of being relevant in any situation you care to mention. We have no need to be afraid of taking on jobs in areas the Church has traditionally shied away from. As Christians, do we believe in walking on the other side and letting Satan do whatever he wants? Today we need to get in there as Christians, to be salt and light in the world just as Jesus first commanded us to be 2,000 years ago. Yes, God does call a few people to serve and equip those who are out working in the world, but they are the exception, not the rule. The rest of us should have our default setting set to working in the nonchurched world. It's there that we can get on with the business of imitating Christ, making friendships with those we meet.

If nothing else, we should be making friendships while we are in secular employment, treating people with dignity and respect. We should be asking God to help out when things get tough instead of running away. The presence of opposition and difficulty is a sure sign that something is going right. Whether we choose to be a shop assistant, a fashion photographer, a teacher or a lawyer, God has a way of using His people for His glory. After all, as servants of the King, we only have a limited amount of borrowed time with which to shine our light in the darkness.

The Spice of Life

Becoming a Christian doesn't mean getting a lobotomy; there are all manner of situations in which we need to use our brains when we sign up for secular employment. We will encounter situations where our values come up against opposition, which puts us in roughly the same position as the believers in the Early Church—and look what they achieved. This is where the unity and community of Christianity come into play. The job of those who are in full-time church work is described in Ephesians 4:11-13:

> It was he who gave some to be apostles, some to be prophets, some to be evangelists, and some to be pastors and teachers, to prepare God's people for works of service, so that the body of Christ may be built up until we all reach unity in the faith and in the knowledge of the Son of God and become mature, attaining to the whole measure of the fullness of Christ.

The reason for handing out all these jobs (leaders, prophets, evangelists, pastors, teachers) is simple: so that the Body of Christ might be built up, that God's people (the saints) might be equipped to serve out there in the world. We can see that the job of an evangelist is not simply to do all the evangelism but also to train the Church to do the evangelism where they're at. The job of a pastor is not simply to pastor everybody in the Church but also to encourage people with pastoral gifts so that they can better encourage others. Those positions in the Church are simply for people who have those gifts in abundance and who are there to equip the Church to do the work. The apostles, prophets, pastors, teachers and evangelists are not the ones who are meant to do the work—that job is for *all* the saints, the people of God.

When we talk about the ministry of this preacher or that worship leader, we should really be evaluating it by looking at the impact it has on those who hear it. The ministry is meant to happen out in the world, not in the Church.

Whose Job Is It Anyway?

We have somehow become confused about what the ministry of a church is. I can remember a well-known evangelist visiting our church many years ago. He was there to "do" our evangelism for a while. All we had to do was bring a couple of *unsaveds* along and let him do the rest. I thought this was great; I could get all my evangelism for the year done in one meeting. It hadn't crossed my mind that I could use him as a tool to equip me to get out there—that would have seemed too much like hard work.

Likewise, the pastor's job is not to pastor everyone; the pastor's job is to make sure that everyone is *pastored*. Thankfully, God seems to be building up leaders who view church very much as a home and a resource, but also as a place to go out from and into the world.

I am excited by the prospect of seeing Christians doing the very best they can do out in the world. The possibilities for a band getting on the charts, for example, and getting out beyond the walls of the church are endless. The opportunities for a nurse to affect the lives of his or her patients and the nurses that he or she works with could also be huge, and equally pleasing to God. The principles are the same whether we are musicians, salespeople, nurses or house cleaners: We do the best we can, celebrate the gifts that God has given us and live lives that are pleasing to God.

Paranoid or Pious?

One sector of the secular world, for example, that has traditionally been the object of much criticism by the Church is the media. An industry that is built on the foundations of greed, image and sex has scared many of us off. Yet those are precisely the reasons why we should be involved in the media, engaging with the culture and influencing the way the rest of the population is molded and taught. If the media has treated Christians harshly in the past, it could be our own fault. As a television director I once met said, "Christians don't need to be so paranoid; there are plenty of open-minded people out there." Those who we consider to be out to persecute us are in the minority.

One of the hopes for revival in these days is that people will start to hear the call and go out and make a difference. The important question in such times is, How do I discover my calling? Many of us get paranoid and worry about missing it or going down the wrong route, as if any error would lead us straight to hell. We remain paralyzed with indecision and end up going nowhere. God is not like that. In one sense He gives us a choice. He hasn't made one narrow, poorly lit path for our lives so that if we should trip up and miss out on being an actor or whatever then we lose the game. Sometimes He gives us choices and says, "Go for it—what's on your heart?"

Obviously, we must be slightly careful on this one; no matter how right it feels, I would view a desire to follow a career as a lap-dancer as a bit suspicious. I recently heard someone describe the way to know what your calling is: when a long-felt desire meets an opportunity. If this happens to you, don't waste time waiting for the heavens to send you your own personal confirmation written in the clouds; give it a try and trust God to shut the doors if it doesn't work out.

This may be all very well if you have a desire to do something or a hunch about where your gifts lie, but for many of us the minute we try to think about the future our minds blank out. Ironically, this is an excellent place in which to be. Think of it as a blank canvas rather than a dead end; pray for God to inspire and install a passion in your heart. If we do believe that God is God, the ultimate creator of all life, then we must believe that everything (and everyone) has a purpose. Even if the situation you find yourself in is bland and uninspiring, it is worth avoiding the temptation to give up on God's calling. As we see in the story of David in the Bible, the seemingly unimpressive can be the most valuable training ground.

Manic Street Preachers

Perhaps by valuing our gifts without covering them with religion—learning how to preach the gospel in the same style as our Savior, who lived a life full of actions, relevant parallels and (in the best possible way) goodness—we will discover a new relationship with the rest of the world. If we weep over the decline of standards and want to have a voice in the world, then we should be involved in it. Shouting from the sidelines was never something that Jesus did. Instead, we should imitate His willingness to establish a relationship with the world. If we do want to be one of the shapers of our culture, we can't expect God to magically transport us, regardless of our training or experience. We need to start at the bottom, like everybody else, with the media studies course, the membership of a political party, the contribution to a local paper or radio station. Alongside that, we need to encourage others to follow these paths and support them as they explore their callings.

The Uncomfortable Pedestal

When we see a Christian in the media or in the political spotlight, we often put that person up on a pedestal and then accuse him or her of selling out and missing opportunities to preach the gospel. Strangely, we don't treat accountants or salespeople the same way; we don't accuse the perfume counter assistant, for example, of losing a potential convert if he or she didn't witness to a customer that made a purchase. Our lives are meant to witness and, where necessary, we are meant to be ready to give our reasons for living life, but not to ram these things down people's throats. God calls some of us to out-and-out evangelism—we see that in the Scriptures; that's what Paul was, an evangelist as well as an apostle and a church planter—but we're all meant to serve the Lord wherever He puts us. I think it's fantastic that nobody is quite certain just how much of a Christian Tony Blair is. He clearly has Christian principles and they influence his work, which suits me fine. I don't need him to do my evangelism for me; I don't need him to be a model to which I can point and say, "Well, Tony's a Christian, so why shouldn't you be one, too?"

God is a big enough reason on His own to follow Him. He doesn't need us down here as His PR people, tackling His oh-so-tricky image problem. What He does need is for us to obey Him and fulfill the potential that He has placed within each of us. He needs us to worship, to listen, to act and to serve. God loves what He has created so much that when we profess our love and desire to serve Him, He has a seemingly limitless set of opportunities for us to explore. What God wants is for us to live the life.

Chapter 14

DOES GOD TAKE VISA?
(A chapter about generosity)

I'm not sure why, but it's easy to feel funny when the subject of money comes up. As a Christian, I get twitchy—nervous even—at the thought of it, as if by bringing it out into the open I admit that I have a problem with it. Like much of our faith, the teaching on it is perfectly clear and simple, but my reaction is pure confusion. The main question—Am I generous enough?—can only ever call up one answer (and it's not yes), but after my sheepish reply come a thousand more questions: How much is enough? Can I give too much? Is it wrong to receive gifts and nice things? Shouldn't I give it all away and live on the street? What do I really need to live on?

A group of us were in South Africa recently, traveling around to different churches, doing meetings and that sort of thing. We saw a lot of wealth, incredible countryside and a lot of poverty. (You can probably tell what's coming next.) But there was a church that we visited that made me completely change my view on giving. As we stood in the poorest church of the trip— a shack in the middle of thousands of other shacks that made up a township called Inanda—we saw people, who had less to live on than we spend each year on movie tickets, giving away all they had. As the pastor announced the start of the collection, I got into my UK Collection Mode: face as miserable as a bald hippie, hands as shy as a monk in a girls' dormitory. I looked around and saw that I was alone in my grumpiness; the church was full of the poorest people I had ever met, giving their money as they danced, sang and cried with joy. They knew, more than I had ever understood, exactly how much God had given them.

No Simple Answers

There are no simple answers to all the questions about giving. There isn't an amount to give that puts us safely in the *generous* category. What we can learn, though, is the attitude. There is a way of life that we see in the Bible that is a perfect model for us to follow.

Acts 2 is one of those passages that we often read in church. At least once a year we dust it off and read all about what happened on the day of Pentecost, what some people call the birthday of the Church. On that day, 120 believers were gathered in an upper room in Jerusalem. They were praying hard because Jesus had told them to wait until the Holy Spirit came, giving them power to be witnesses in Jerusalem, Judea, Samaria and to the ends of the earth. Finally, the day came and the Holy Spirit turned up, shaking the place up and bringing with Him what seemed like tongues of fire. Straight away, the believers were filled with the Spirit, and they began to speak in other languages. They went into the streets and were met by large crowds—who thought they were drunk, they seemed so happy—who were even more confused that these uneducated men could suddenly speak a variety of languages. Peter preached the gospel, and at the end he told them that he and the other 119 believers weren't drunk, as the crowd had thought, but full of the Spirit of God. Three thousand people became Christians on the spot.

The story doesn't stop there. Being a bit of a showman, I was kind of disappointed when I first read this passage. *How*, I scoffed to myself, *did they ever think they would top that? Everybody knows that you save your best gags till last.* As I read on, I stopped criticizing. The best bit follows, as it describes life after that day:

> They devoted themselves to the apostles' teaching and to the fellowship, to the breaking of bread and to prayer. Everyone was filled with awe, and many wonders and miraculous signs were done by the apostles. All the believers were together and had everything in common. Selling their possessions and goods, they gave to anyone as he had need. Every day they continued to meet together in the temple courts. They broke bread in their homes and ate together with glad and sincere hearts, praising God and enjoying the favor of all the people. And the Lord added to their number daily those who were being saved (Acts 2:42-47).

What we might call the fruit of the Holy Spirit's visit to the believers—the way that it changed their lives—was that these people devoted themselves to the apostles' teaching. They became a group who were committed to teaching and to fellowship, to breaking bread and to praying. They had everything in common—that doesn't mean that they all immediately liked the same kind of music or food—they simply sold their possessions and gave the proceeds away.

The first fruit of Pentecost was that the gospel was preached powerfully. There was a display of God's supernatural power that blew people's minds and opened their eyes. But what we are left with is not simply the class of A.D. 30, a group of spiritual junkies talking about the glory days of the ultimate rush. What they were left with was a desire to be more generous, to be more like God.

The Scriptures are full of encouragement for us to be more like God in our generosity. He keeps on giving, never stopping to rest or to stock up on blessings for Himself or to check out what's happening on the other channels. God is love, and the nature of love is to give itself away. Look at the Bible and it isn't hard to find examples of God giving to His people: He gives protection, freedom, children, healing and more. The biggest example has to be Jesus, the most precious and valuable thing that God had. The act of sending down His most precious child is the blueprint for us, a perfect model of how to live our lives. Jesus knew this, and in the Sermon on the Mount He told the disciples to "Give, and it will be given to you. A good measure, pressed down, shaken together and running over, will be poured into your lap" (Luke 6:38). Jesus also encouraged the disciples to be the kind of people who would give their time, money and possessions as part of their worship.

In his second letter to the Corinthians, Paul says that God loves a cheerful giver (see 2 Cor. 9:7). The Greek word for "cheerful" literally means "hilarious." God doesn't just want us to give; He wants us to give with joy and with hilarity. God took great delight when Joash put a chest outside the temple courts. All of the officials and people brought their contributions gladly, dropping them into the chest until it was full (see 2 Chron. 24:10). The key word here is "gladly" (or "cheerfully"). In our society, we are meant to be a prophetic people. That isn't a flowery way of saying that we need to shout at people while they wait their turn at the supermarket checkout line, nor does it mean that we are to cultivate the personal hygiene of a confused skunk. It means that we are supposed to show a different way by our actions.

The churchgoers of Inanda showed me something by their actions. As they gave cheerfully, their actions told me that when it comes to possessions, attitude is everything. In a society whose people are so hung up on what they can get, what they would do with a lottery jackpot, how much can be saved (or spent) each year, or whether investments move up or down by a fraction of a percent, we as God's people must learn to live a different way and develop a different attitude toward ownership. Tightly holding on to possessions is not God's way. When we see poverty, we should give; when we see loneliness, we should be offering hospitality. These things are signs that God is alive, among us and interested in the world.

Tight Fists or Holy Hands?

There have been many talks given in church about steward-ship, looking after God's money and resources. Sometimes I understand what they mean: being wise about how we spend money, making sure that it isn't all blown on a night out in Vegas for the pastoral staff. At other times, though, steward-ship is just another word for being tight-fisted. God has plen-ty of cash and is the ultimate in generosity. Can you, after all, seriously imagine anybody being more generous than God? He doesn't want us to be mean with our possessions, looking after them so carefully in case someone steals them. He wants us to be willing to give away most of what we have.

What It's All About

A couple of years ago at the Soul Survivor conference, Steve Chalke spoke at one of the main evening meetings. He tack-led the subject of justice, challenging people to be offended by poverty and motivated to do something about it. At the end, he invited each person to go back to his or her tent and find an item of clothing that he or she wanted to give away to homeless people in London. People lined up in silence to give away what they had chosen. After 30 minutes, there was a truck full of clothes heading back to London.

I thought long and hard about that night. There was something in the atmosphere that made the occasion special. On the face of it, it was different from putting coins or bills in a collection box, but there was such a hush as the people lined up that the meeting became different. I soon realized what had happened: People weren't giving their clothes to the homeless (they knew nothing about them and Steve had only mentioned them at the end of his talk); they were giving to God. It was one of the most intimate worship times I have ever experienced.

Yes, it is a good thing to be giving money away to the Church, to the poor, to charities; but as the story shows, the object of our giving really isn't the Church, the poor or charities—it is God. When we give, we do it because God wants us to, because it pleases Him. He gave us, free of charge, the life of His only Son. That is what we respond to when our hand goes to our pocket, regardless of who ends up getting the cash. We are being like God and responding to His grace.

Mine vs. God's

The secret of giving generously is to realize that it all belongs to God in the first place. When we become Christians, a transaction takes place: We give our lives to God and He pays for them on the Cross. When He bought us, it wasn't like a home assembly piece of furniture with half the parts missing. He got the whole kit, every part of our lives. He bought our finances, our clothes, homes, abilities and dreams. Every bit of us belongs to God.

It's great when we see things this way; it makes it so much easier for God to shift His possessions around. Three years ago, a couple whom I had never met came up to me and said that God had told them to give me their car. I was amazed. My car had broken down that week and I was about to arrange a suitable funeral for it. I was convinced that they were messing around, but they promised me they weren't. Then I realized what was going on: They were obviously about to give me their old beat-up failure of a car, easing their consciences as they eased into the soft leather of their new BMW. But I thought it would be worth my while to have a look, and there was no reason I couldn't sell it for scrap and walk away with $50 in my pocket.

The couple took me around the corner and pointed to what I can only describe as a *successful man's car*. This was the sort of car that you drove if you had an Armani suit hanging in the back. It was a car that said, "Yes, I do have lots of credit cards, a six-foot-wide fridge and a stomach the size of Texas." I liked it.

"The Lord bless you," I said, trying my best not to go up and kiss it. I couldn't believe that they were giving it to me, but they said God that had told them to do so, and as far as they were concerned that was all that needed to be said.

I thanked them over and over, wondering whether they might expect me to do something in return, like keep it clean.

"The way I see it," the man said, "is that it's just like a chess board; God owns all the pieces and He's just moving them around."

This was an amazing experience. Not only did I end up with a car that suited my waist size, but I also received a clear sign from God through His people that He loves and cares for me.

Right now you might be feeling a bit confused. How can I be banging on about giving it all away in one breath and drooling over a Vauxhall Carlton CD 2000 (ABS braking, CD player, power-assisted steering) in the next? I'm not sure either, but I do know that God loves to give gifts. Before Jesus was even out of diapers, He was given a range of exclusive and expensive gifts. Even living your whole life for Jesus doesn't repay the price He paid for all of us on the cross.

Perhaps the answer lies within us. We are all different, all in different situations with different levels of wealth. Apart from maybe two people in this world, we all know someone who is better off and someone who is worse off than us. What we can all do, though, is give. I'm into the discipline of tithing, giving away 10 percent of whatever I have; but I think it's wrong that once we've given God His tenth we think we can get on with the business of enjoying our 90 percent. Instead, I think it's better to ask God how much of His money we can keep. We belong to Him, and everything that we have and everything that we are belongs to Him too.

Done this way, being generous can really hurt. When we get to the stage when giving is painful, we know we're headed in the right direction. While we may never get there— never be able to sit back and say, "Yes, I give enough"—we will at least be facing in the right direction.

Yes, but Does God Take Visa?

Today, things like telephone banking, the Internet and credit cards make looking after and getting rid of cash something that can happen in an instant. Giving to God can seem a bit less convenient, a bit more of a hassle. Remembering to take money along to church is sometimes as hard as remembering to take the Bible. There are a million obstacles that block our path and countless excuses to turn around and head home, giving up on the discipline of being generous, going soft on giving to God. "Come into my life, Lord," we say, and we show Him around the place for the first time. We give Him the full tour—memories, loves, pains and hopes—but quickly walk past the box in the corner where we stash the cash.

We won't think twice about grabbing a McDonald's value meal gone large, but putting the equivalent cash in the collection basket can give us worse indigestion than a truckload of moldy fishburgers. Listlessly handing over the money on a Sunday seems so dull, so low on fun, that there is little doubt that we struggle with it.

Jesus said in Matthew 10:38 that if anyone was up for following Him, they had to take up their Cross. That means putting down whatever else we're playing with and committing ourselves to going His way. Daily. This is what stops Christianity from being a fluffy, cuddly, sweet and lovely fortnight break, and takes it to the next level. This is what stopped the post-Pentecost Church from being a bunch of lazy morons and turned them into a group that changed the world. When God has it all from us, Christianity becomes something that is real and effective. We need to give more than just our money; we need to learn to live generously with everything we have—time, energy, wisdom and love.

The Bible is filled with teachings on wealth and poverty. In the Old Testament, it is the second most common topic after idolatry. In the New Testament, there are more than 500 verses of direct teaching on the subject; that's an incredible

1 in 16 verses. Jesus talked more about wealth and poverty than He did about heaven and hell, sexual morality, the Law or the Second Coming. In James's letter, 1 in every 5 verses is about the relationship between the rich and the poor; in Luke's Gospel, it is 1 in every 7. In Mary's song (see Luke 1:46-55), she says that with the coming of Jesus the mighty will be brought low, the rich sent away empty, the poor exalted and the hungry satisfied. So why do we talk about money so much? We talk about it because money is one of the biggest issues in the Bible.

The first Christians were people of mercy, giving to all who were in need. The believers in Jesus were known as "the people of the way" before they were known as Christians. This was because of the way that they lived. They weren't called the people of the belief, the people of the experience or the people of the party, but the people of the way. People will see a difference in us when we learn to be generous, when we give when it hurts. It's part of our worship and it's part of our witness.

This chapter started with me moaning about generosity being such a difficult issue to understand. I hope we've finished in a better place. There are no simple answers; that much is true, but there is a rule: If it isn't hurting, it's not giving. At the end of the day, we've all been given so much that there are a thousand ways that we can give back to God. At some point it gets down to the subject of money, but before that it's all about attitude—to God, to others and to those consumer goods that make life just a little bit more comfortable.

Having a lifestyle of giving breaks the hold of materialism over us. Materialism is essentially loving and putting your security in money and possessions. Jesus tells us to make sure that we store treasures in heaven and not on Earth (see Matt. 6:19-20). This means that we are to live on Earth with heaven in mind, and not our bank balance. We set our hearts on money and possessions not only because of greed and selfishness but also because of insecurity and anxiety. Giving generously breaks the power of these things over our lives. A life of generosity says loud and clear, "I trust God to look after me." It is to know that every hair on our heads has been counted by Him. To give is to find freedom.

Be like Jesus—give your life away.

Chapter 15

HOW TO KEEP GOING
(A chapter about persevering)

Other people always seem to have this whole Christianity thing a good deal more figured out than I do. Since I was first eased into my spiritual diapers, I had a knack for checking out the person up front and thinking one simple thought: *I hate you.* While that person might enlighten audiences with heart-wrenching tales of personal torment and tragedy, my response would be a self-righteous "Pah! You think you've had it hard?" In my own defense, I could list numerous reasons why my situation was a worse deal than his or hers; although most of these reasons came down to the simple fact that he or she was up there on stage and I was down in the crowd and none of it was at all fair. At the very heart of my confusion was a blindness to the fact that God moves in mysterious ways, unimpressed by those things that we seem to get so hung up about (like fame and recognition), yet very interested in the things that we often dismiss as belonging to the bottom of the spiritual pile (like servant-heartedness and attitude).

Jesus said that He made His way down here so that we might have life and have it in all its fullness (see John 10:10). It wasn't His intention that we spend our time limping around, enduring a second-rate existence. My problem was that I took this to mean that we were to get exactly what we wanted, when we wanted. As we have hopefully seen throughout this book, the life that God values is not necessarily one marked out by the glitz and glamour of our misinterpretations of success.

In a strange way, my whining in the general direction of God and those who had "made it in life" prevented me from actually doing anything about my own life. I was enjoying much the same role as the competitive father who screams from the sidelines as his youngest child plays in the Under 11 soccer; getting out there and doing something was just not an option. Perhaps the root of it all was a mistaken belief that "abundant life" meant an abundance of my kind of good things, when what it really means is a true and full relationship with God as Father, Savior and Creator of the world. Perhaps if I had worked as hard as I could to reach the goal, I would have come up against another problem (one that sadly affects many more Christians than we would like to admit): the temptation to either sell out, burn out or fade out.

Our relationship with our Creator is often talked about in terms of a journey. We have all been encouraged to run the race and to keep on pressing toward the prize (see 1 Cor. 9:24), but just how much do we realize that we are taking part in a marathon and not a sprint? The prize does not go to the person who makes the most progress in the shortest time, nor does it go to whoever falls over and barks the most. At the end of the day we will be standing face to face with God, and I want to know Him as well as possible by that time. It is important that we prepare ourselves to run the marathon, to go all the way and not give up.

King David made sure that we had a top-notch example of long-term commitment and development. Through his story in the Old Testament, we see great accomplishments and tremendous mistakes. Despite falling in ways that many of us can relate to, David was still described as being a man after God's heart. Despite tripping over the hurdles with such incredible style, he got up and he kept going. What was the key to his success? I believe that it is essentially very simple: He finished well because he started well.

Before We Get to David

I became a Christian when I was 15 and, as I mentioned earlier, I wanted to do church work from that moment on. Between the ages of 15 and 29, there was large gap in my life. At times I waited patiently; at other times I got annoyed. I was sure my calling was out there; there was just a small matter of getting it to me that needed to be sorted out. As a consequence, I put very little effort into my other activities during that time. I was disinterested at school, lethargic at University and vague when I got to work. I wish now that I had done more with those years and used them in preparation for the future, whatever that was going to contain.

I know a man named James Ryle who pastors a church in Denver, Colorado. James spent his early days as a Christian a little differently from the way I spent mine. At the time of his conversion, he was serving a sentence for involuntary man-slaughter as the result of a car accident in which a passenger of his died. While James was in prison, he used his time to read the Bible from cover to cover and devoured whole chunks of the dictionary to improve his vocabulary. He knew that when he got out he was going to do something to com-municate the truth about Jesus to other people. Because of his vision, James used his time wisely. It would have been easy for him to spend those years in jail feeling that his life was rotting away, being wasted while he could be doing so much more with it. Today, James is still reaping the benefit of those years of disciplined preparation.

David Was a Little Shepherd Boy

In a culture where the older you were the better, especially in comparison to your siblings, David did not get off to a flying start; he was number eight of Jesse's sons. One day, his fam-ily received a visit to their home in Bethlehem from the prophet Samuel. The prophet was visiting as a result of what he believed God had told him: One of Jesse's sons was to be anointed as the new king over Israel. Samuel told Jesse to consecrate himself and his sons and to accompany him to the sacrifice. When Jesse and sons arrived, Samuel saw Eliab, Jesse's eldest, and thought to himself that he had to be the future king. It did not occur to him that anyone other than the eldest son would be in line for the job.

> But the LORD said to Samuel, "Do not consider his appearance or his height, for I have rejected him. The LORD does not look at the things man looks at. Man looks at the outward appearance, but the LORD looks at the heart" (1 Sam. 16:7).

That happens to be one of my favorite verses in Scripture. We all place so much value on external appearances, judging people on all sorts of criteria from age and beauty to style and class. What God was actually saying was that His values are less superficial than ours. It is important to note that God did not reject Eliab as a person—He loved Eliab as one of His children—He just rejected him as king over Israel.

The Bible goes on to say that later, after all of Jesse's sons had been presented to Samuel (and subsequently rejected), Samuel asked Jesse whether there were any more sons for him to look at. "'There is still the youngest,' Jesse answered, 'but he is tending the sheep'" (1 Sam. 16:11)

It amazes me that Jesse didn't even say his name. It was as if he thought his son's chances of ever being more than a shepherd were so slim that he not only didn't trouble Samuel by bringing David along, but he also didn't bother saying his son's name. So Samuel told Jesse to send for David. When David arrived, the Lord told Samuel that his search was over and to anoint David at once. Imagine, one minute David is tending his flock, and the next he finds himself anointed as king over all Israel. Then, as if none of that was strange enough, he returns to the fields and gets on with the job of being a shepherd boy. (We know this because in 1 Samuel 16:19, after the anointing, it says, "Then Saul sent messengers to Jesse and said, 'Send me your son David, who is with the sheep.'")

Call me fussy, but life as a sheep-nanny would not be my first choice to prepare me as direct ruler over all Israel. I would make sure that I was well accustomed to a life of luxury before it ever became an official duty. David, on the other hand, went back to his old life, carrying on as before with his boring, lonely and unnoticed job. Whenever I have been doing something that fulfils that criteria, I have found it nearly impossible to resist the temptation to slack off and do something else. The temptation has been to confuse a dull, unappreciated task with a lack of spiritual kudos. Put another way, doing the more public and esteemed jobs often seems to be so right and "of the Lord." Study, work and preparation may not seem related to the job of our dreams—at times being a shepherd may not have made much sense to David—but God often uses people who have prepared, calling those who have not wasted their present by whining about the future.

What did David do when he was looking after the sheep? I think he got to know his God. All the indications are that he spent those lonely nights in prayer, communicating with God and developing their relationship. The backdrop to this friendship was the raw earth, the hills and the desert. David reflected this in his psalms, writing about the God he met in the mountains, the wind and the sky. Through contemplating the products of God's creativity and by spending time in prayer, David made sure that his time was not wasted.

Also, it seems from Scripture that David was great on the harp (see 1 Sam. 16:18). Now, we may be in danger of reading a little too much into the text with this, but it is not hard to imagine what sort of reaction David might have gotten from his seven elder brothers when he practiced at home. This leads nicely into the conclusion that David spent a fair amount of his scale and harmony writing time out in the desert. As well as music, he worked on the psalms—originally written as lyrics—and developed his talents. Again, we see that his time was not wasted but used wisely to hone skills that would later lead many to develop their own relationship with God.

David found opportunity to put his faith into action. He made sure that he backed up his shepherding career with more than just study and prayer; when he had to, David was ready to leap in and defend his flock (see 1 Sam. 17:34-35).

The Great Unveiling

The story of David's encounter with Goliath in 1 Samuel 17 reads like a grand unveiling of *The David Project*. During this encounter, David will display all of the attributes that he has diligently worked on away from public view and praise. At the time, the giant was taunting his enemies, and no one in Israel would accept his challenge (see vv. 8-11). David's initial task, set by his father, was to take provisions to his brothers (note the liberal spread of irony with the word provisions—God provided them with, in the shape of David, far more than they hoped for). When David arrived at the camp, he was surprised to find that Goliath's threats went unanswered and offered to resolve the situation himself. In response, Saul questioned David's age and experience in the light of the giant's abilities (see vv. 17,32-33).

What was David's knockout answer to convince Saul and everyone else that he could fight this huge, hardened soldier?

"Your servant has been keeping his fathers sheep" (vv. 34).

I am not sure they would have been convinced.

David continued: "When a lion or a bear came and carried off a sheep from the flock, I went after it, struck it and rescued the sheep from its mouth. When it turned on me, I seized it by its hair, struck it and killed it. Your servant has killed both the lion and the bear; this uncircumcised Philistine will be like one of them, because he has defied the armies of the living God. The Lord who delivered me from the paw of the lion and the paw of the bear will deliver me from the hand of this Philistine" (vv. 34-37).

This was David's graduation. All that he had learned when surrounded by sheep was clear to see. He displayed trust, faith and wisdom beyond both his social standing and his years. His boring, lonely and unnoticed job had taught him well and had trained him for a conflict he could never have predicted. Yet he knew that Goliath would be the same as a bear or a lion; he knew this because he had killed the beasts before and because his relationship with his Creator was deep enough to back up his hunch that what he was about to do was right.

It would have been easy for David to wonder why he was looking after sheep when he had been anointed as king over Israel. Surely that made him too important to look after a flock of sheep? Looking at our own situation, we may feel indignant that we are not at a massive church, leading, teaching or doing something else to entertain the masses with our particular gifting. Perhaps we may feel that as our place is on stage, we won't busy ourselves with those menial tasks done by people who don't get up on the stage. Time and time again, people have discovered that God, like a wise father, trusts people with the small things before He moves them on to the bigger ones.

David learned his lessons well, despite the fact that he must have wondered how God was going to engineer a career change from shepherd boy to reigning monarch. It seems slightly unlikely that his to-do list contained the instruction: Practice slaying large animals just in case you ever meet a big Philistine. His task was to be faithful in the small, to be obedient in a present that seemed divorced from ambition. As David lived his own life, God made sure that he received full preparation for an unpredictable future. Like David, we could do well to learn not to waste the moment, to express our love for Jesus by serving Him when there is nobody around to watch. If we can learn to deliver the goods when ours is an audience of One, if we can learn to value the approval of God more than that of man, then it will be immaterial whether 10 or 10,000 people see us at work.

Enjoy the Silence

Maybe there's a reason why so many of us cry out for company. Perhaps the presence of pain and hurt inside demands the presence of people around us, taking the focus off that with which we need to deal and placing it on others. I spent a long time avoiding issues buried deep within by never really being alone. I knew that there would be considerable pain waiting for me when I faced my issues, but it was only when I was alone and facing things that God could actually help me. Many of David's psalms reflect the solitude of his job, and many echo the cry that comes from deep within us when we are faced with pain: Where are You, God? It is a great thing to have fellowship, to hang out with and enjoy time with others, but not as a substitute for spending time with God in solitude, allowing Him to search us and find anything that does not reflect His purity.

This is the bit where I risk sounding like a very old and dull person, but life can sometimes get boring—it was for David and it is for us. The temptation is to confuse monotony with a lack of spirituality (this job is dull, so God can't be in it), and to equate those gooey rushes of emotion with an abundance of spirituality (I fell over 17 times at church today and it felt great). The quest for a deeper relationship with God and the quest for a more explosive encounter with Him are traveling in two separate directions. To hanker for one high after another will result in a crisis of disillusionment when the realization hits that God likes us close, attentive and obedient. We need to learn to stick things out because perseverance comes very high on the list of things that God loves, choosing as He does to develop many things in us through it.

James 1:2-3 is a favorite of mine, carrying the immortal message that we should "consider it pure joy . . . [to] face trials of many kinds, because you know that the testing of your faith develops perseverance." I have seen loads of people who started well and had plenty of gifts, but who have fallen by the wayside simply because they have not known how to keep going. They thought that they had signed up for a 100-meter sprint, but then found out that they were in a marathon. I have seen others who at the beginning were fairly unimpressive on the outside, yet kept plodding on in their relationship with God. Such training has produced strong and healthy Christians.

The Power of the Plodder

Some friends and I once asked Steve Chalke what he thought his greatest asset was. I was fairly sure that his personality, broadcasting experience or good looks would come pretty high on the list. He really shocked me when he said, "I'm a plodder. Whether things are good or bad, I just keep going."

I remember hearing someone say once that God is not looking so much for great ability in us, or even credibility with others, but our availability to Him. We need to learn to be available to Him all the time. God looks not for superstars but for servants. He looks for people who will follow Him for as long as it takes and wherever it goes.

Now I am a great, true and genuine supporter of the Manchester United soccer club. It is well known by my friends that I can recite the team's starting line-up since 1973 and often like to practice this among them on long journeys. I once read an interview with former Manchester United player David Beckham in which he was asked what he thought it was that had made him a Premier League player. Like the man himself, his answer was short yet totally accurate: practice. As a child, he would spend hours kicking a ball against a wall or playing with his dad. We too need to practice. We need to give our spirituality the chance to develop from clumsy infancy to skilled adulthood. We need to seek God with all that we have, especially when there appears to be nothing in it for us, except Him.

At the beginning of this book we talked about worship, which is the search of God. We want to finish by saying that to truly live life is to pursue God with all our hearts, following Him with everything that we have, obeying Him in the most menial and unnoticed of tasks. Our spiritual life is meant to be like an iceberg: The visible tip should be 10 percent of what is below the surface of the water. We could do well to develop the 90 percent of our lives before God and God only. Through that exercise of perseverance comes righteousness and a deeper relationship with Him. That way, later on in life we won't sell out; we will learn that when prosperity comes to us in marriage or a career, we won't sell out to the world because we will have been trained to value the completion of the race more highly than the view along the way. Likewise, we won't burn out. We will pace ourselves, learn to keep going and see it through to the end. We won't fade out like those who start well but whose enthusiasm for God gradually dims, because ours will be a spirituality that perseveres.